Holt McDougal
Mathematics

Course 2
Problem Solving
Workbook

a division of Houghton Mifflin Harcourt

Contents

Holt McDougal Mathematics

LESSON 1-1 Problem Solving
Numbers and Patterns

Write the correct answer.

1. Trains leave Peapack station at 7:00 A.M., 7:16 A.M., 7:32 A.M., and 7:48 A.M. Assume that the pattern continues. If you arrive at the station at 8:30 A.M., at what time will the next scheduled train leave?

_____

2. Suppose the pattern 8, 16, 24, 32, ... is continued forever. Will the number 174 appear in the pattern? Why or why not?

_____

3. A water tank holding 100 gallons begins to leak at 6:00 P.M. At 7:00 P.M. the tank has 94 gallons. At 8:00 P.M the tank has 88 gallons. At 9:00 P.M. the tank has 82 gallons. If the pattern continues, how many gallons will be left at 11:00 P.M.?

_____

4. Awilda is making a necklace with sphere, pyramid, and cube shaped beads. If she continues the pattern below, what are the shapes of the next five beads?

Choose the letter for the best answer.

5. The drawing at the right shows the first three figures in a pattern. If the pattern continues, how many circles will be in the fifth figure of the pattern?

   A 20   C 27

   B 24   D 35

6. The table shows the number of handshakes if each person in a group shakes each other's hand once. How many handshakes will there be if there are 9 people?

   F 20   H 36

   G 30   J 45

7. Melissa wrote the following number pattern: 71, 66, 59, 50, 39, ... What is the next number in the pattern?

   A 26   C 30

   B 27   D 35

Figure 1   Figure 2   Figure 3

People	2	3	4	5	6
Number of Handshakes	1	3	6	10	15

8. By July 1, Bob saved $120. By July 8, he saved $185. By July 15, Bob saved $250. If the pattern continues, how much will he have saved by July 29?

   F $315   H $390

   G $380   J $415

LESSON 1-2 Problem Solving
Exponents

Write the correct answer.

1. The cells of the bacteria *E. coli* can double every 20 minutes. If you begin with a single cell, how many cells can there be after 4 hours?

_____

2. The population of metropolitan Orlando, Florida, has doubled about every 16 years since 1960. In 2000, the population was 1,644,561. At this doubling rate, what could the population be in 2048?

_____

3. A prizewinner can choose Prize A, $2,000 per year for 15 years, or Prize B, 3 cents the first year, with the amount tripling each year through the fifteenth year. Which prize is more valuable? How much is it worth?

_____

4. Maria had triplets. Each of her 3 children had triplets. If the pattern continued for 2 more generations, how many great-great-grandchildren would Maria have?

_____

Choose the letter for the best answer.

5. A theory states that the CPU clock speed in a computer doubles every 18 months. If the clock speed was 33 MHz in 1991, how can you use exponents to find out how fast the clock speed is after doubling 3 times?

   A 33^3

   B $3^2 \cdot 33$

   C $2^3 \cdot 33$

   D 33^2

6. The classroom is a square with a side length of 13 feet and an area of 169 square feet. How can you write the area in exponential form?

   F 2^{13}

   G 13^2

   H 3^{13}

   J 13^3

7. In 2000, Wake County, North Carolina, had a population of 610,284. This is about twice the population in 1980. If the county grows at the same rate every 20 years, what will its population be in 2040?

   A 915,426

   B 1,220,568

   C 1,830,852

   D 2,441,136

8. The number of cells of a certain type of bacteria doubles every 45 minutes. If you begin with a single cell, how many cells could there be after 6 hours?

   F 64

   G 256

   H 360

   J 540

Holt McDougal Mathematics

Problem Solving

LESSON 1-3

Scientific Notation

Write the correct answer.

1. Earth is about 150,000,000 kilometers from the sun. Write this distance in scientific notation.

2. The planet Neptune is about 4.5×10^9 kilometers from the sun. Write this distance in standard form.

3. At the end of 2004, the U.S. federal debt was about $7 trillion, 600 billion. Write the amount of the debt in standard form and in scientific notation.

4. Canada is about 1.0×10^7 square kilometers in size. Brazil is about 8,500,000 square kilometers in size. Which country has a greater area?

Choose the letter for the best answer.

5. China's population in 2001 was approximately 1,273,000,000. Mexico's population for the same year was about 1.02×10^8. How much greater was China's population than Mexico's?

   A 1,375,000,000

   B 1,274,020,000

   C 1,171,000,000

   D 102,000,000

6. In mid-2001, the world population was approximately 6.137×10^9. By 2050, the population is projected to be 9.036×10^9. By how much will world population increase?

   F 151,730,000

   G 289,900,000

   H 1,517,300,000

   J 2,899,000,000

7. The Alpha Centauri star system is about 4.3 light-years from Earth. One light-year, the distance light travels in 1 year, is about 6 trillion miles. About how many miles away from Earth is Alpha Centauri?

   A 2.58×10^{13} miles

   B 6×10^{13} miles

   C 1.03×10^{12} miles

   D 2.58×10^9 miles

8. In the fall of 2001, students in Columbia, South Carolina, raised $440,000 to buy a new fire truck for New York City. If the money had been collected in pennies, how many pennies would that have been?

   F 4.4×10^6

   G 4.4×10^5

   H 4.4×10^7

   J 4.4×10^8

Holt McDougal Mathematics

Problem Solving

Order of Operations

Write the correct answer.

1. In 1975, the minimum wage was $2.10 per hour. Write and simplify an expression to show wages earned in a 35-hour week after a $12 tax deduction.

2. George bought 3 boxes of Girl Scout cookies at $3.50 per box and 4 boxes at $3.00 per box. Write and simplify an expression to show his total cost.

3. In 1 week Ed works 4 days, 3 hours a day, for $12 per hour, and 2 days, 6 hours a day, for $15 per hour. Simplify the expression $12(4 \cdot 3) + 15(2 \cdot 6)$ to find Ed's weekly earnings.

4. Keisha had $150. She bought jeans for $27, a sweater for $32, 3 blouses for $16 each, and 2 pairs of socks for $6 each. Simplify the expression $150 - [27 + 32 + (3 \cdot 16) + (2 \cdot 6)]$ to find out how much money she has left.

Choose the letter for the best answer.

5. As of September 1, 1997, the minimum wage was set at $5.15 per hour. How much more would someone earn now than in 1997 if she earns $5 more per hour for a 40-hour week?

   A $206 more

   B $200 more

   C $406 more

   D $400 more

6. Gary received $200 in birthday gifts. He bought 5 CDs for $15 each, 2 posters for $12 each, and a $70 jacket. How much money does he have left?

   F $31

   G $10

   H $132

   J $169

7. Yvonne took her younger brother and his friends to the movies. She bought 5 tickets for $8 each, 4 drinks for $2 each, and two $3 containers of popcorn. How much did she spend?

   A $22

   B $51

   C $54

   D $38

8. On a business trip, Mr. Chang stayed in a hotel for 7 nights. He paid $149 per night. While he was there, he made 8 phone calls at $2 each and charged $81 to room service. How much did he spend?

   F $246

   G $946

   H $1,043

   J $1,140

Holt McDougal Mathematics

Problem Solving
Properties of Numbers

Write the correct answer.

1. Jo makes and sells jewelry. She sold three bracelets for $45, $17, and $25. Write an expression for the total Jo received. Explain how you can use properties and mental math to simplify the expression.

_____

_____

_____

2. Use parentheses to show two ways of grouping the numbers in 12 • 8 • 25. Tell which expression you think would be easier to simplify, and why. Then simplify the expression.

_____

_____

_____

3. The distance from Mark's apartment to his job is 27 miles. Mark works 5 days per week. How many miles does Mark drive to and from work each week?

_____

4. Jane said that 6(64) = 6(50) + 6(14). Is she correct? Use the Distributive Property to explain your answer.

_____

_____

_____

Choose the letter for the best answer.

5. Maxine works 8 hours at a rate of $16 per hour. Which expression could **not** be used to find her total earnings in dollars?

   A 8 • (10 • 6)

   B 8 • (20 − 4)

   C 8 • (10 + 6)

   D 8 • (8 + 8)

6. Rosemary runs 16 miles on Friday, 8 miles on Saturday, and 14 miles on Sunday. How many miles does Rosemary run in all?

   F 22 mi

   G 24 mi

   H 30 mi

   J 38 mi

7. Which of the following represents the Identity Property?

   A (8 • 4) • 3 = 8 • (4 • 3)

   B 16 • 0 = 0

   C 25 • 1 = 25

   D 6(26) = 6(20) + 6(6)

8. Which of the following shows how the Distributive Property could be used to simplify 7(28)?

   F 7 • 2 • 8

   G 7 • (20 • 8)

   H 7 • (20 + 8)

   J (7 • 20) + 8

LESSON	# Problem Solving
1-6	*Variables and Algebraic Expressions*

Write the correct answer.

1. In 2000, people in the United States watched television an average of 29 hours per week. Use the expression $29w$ for $w = 4$ to find out about how many hours per month this is.

   _____

2. Find the value of the variable w in the expression $29w$ to find the average number of hours people watched television in a year. Find the value of the expression.

   _____

3. The expression $y + 45$ gives the year when a person will be 45 years old, where y is the year of birth. When will a person born in 1992 be 45 years old?

   _____

4. The expression $24g$ gives the number of miles Guy's car can travel on g gallons of gas. If the car has 6 gallons of gas left, how much farther can he drive?

   _____

Choose the letter for the best answer.

5. Sam is 5 feet tall. The expression $0.5m + 60$ can be used to calculate his height in inches if he grows an average of 0.5 inch each month. How tall will Sam be in 6 months?

   A 56 inches

   B 5 feet 6 inches

   C 63 inches

   D 53 inches

6. The winner of the 1911 Indianapolis 500 auto race drove at a speed of about $s - 56$ mi/h, where s is the 2001 winning speed of about 131 mi/h. What was the approximate winning speed in 1911?

   F 75 mi/h

   G 186 mi/h

   H 85 mi/h

   J 187 mi/h

7. The expression $1,587v$ gives the number of pounds of waste produced per person in the United States in v years. How many pounds of waste per person is produced in the United States in 6 years?

   A 1,581 pounds

   B 1,593 pounds

   C 9,348 pounds

   D 9,522 pounds

8. The expression $\$1.25p + \$3.50$ can be used to calculate the total charge for faxing p pages at a business services store. How much would it cost to fax 8 pages?

   F $12.50

   G $4.75

   H $13.50

   J $10.00

Holt McDougal Mathematics

LESSON
1-7

Problem Solving
Translating Words into Math

Write the correct answer.

1. Employers in the United States allocate *n* fewer vacation days than the 25 days given by the average Japanese employer. Write an algebraic expression to show the number of vacation days given U.S. workers.

   _____

2. There are 112 members in the Somerset Marching Band. They will march in *r* equal rows. Write an algebraic expression for the number of band members in each row.

3. A cup of cottage cheese has 26 grams of protein. Write an algebraic expression for the amount of protein in *s* cups of cottage cheese.

   _____

4. Every morning Sasha exercises for 20 minutes. She exercises *k* minutes every evening. Next week she will double her exercise time at night. Write an algebraic expression to show how long Sasha will exercise each day next week.

   _____

Choose the letter for the best answer.

5. One centimeter equals 0.3937 inches. Which algebraic expression shows how many inches are in *c* centimeters?

   A $0.3937 + c$

   B $0.3937 \div c$

   C $c \div 0.3937$

   D $0.3937c$

6. In 1957, the Soviet Union launched *Sputnik 1,* the first satellite to orbit Earth. It circled Earth every 1.6 hours for 92 days, then burned up. If the satellite traveled *m* miles per hour, which algebraic expression shows the length of the orbit?

   F $92m$

   G $1.6m$

   H $m \div 1.6$

   J $92 \div m$

7. Gina's heart rate is 70 beats per minute. Which algebraic expression shows the number of beats in *h* hours?

   A $70h$

   B $60h$

   C $4,200h$

   D $3,600h$

8. The Harris family went on vacation for *w* weeks and 3 days. Which algebraic expression shows the total number of days of their vacation?

   F $7w$

   G $3w$

   H $7w + 3$

   J $3w + 7$

LESSON	**Problem Solving**
1-8	*Simplifying Algebraic Expressions*

Write the correct answer. Use the figures for Problems 1–3.

1. Figure 1 shows the length of each side of a garden. Write and simplify an expression for the perimeter of the garden.

_____

2. Figure 2 is a square swimming pool. Write and simplify an expression for the perimeter of the pool.

_____

3. Write and simplify an expression for the combined perimeter of the garden and the pool.

_____

_____

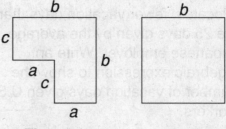

Figure 1   **Figure 2**

4. The Pantheon in Rome has n granite columns in each of 3 rows. Write and simplify an addition expression to show the number of columns. Then evaluate the expression for $n = 8$.

_____

_____

Choose the letter for the best answer.

5. Which is an expression that shows the earnings of a telemarketer who worked for 23 hours at a salary of d dollars per hour?

   A $d + 23$ C $d \div 23$

   B $23d$ D $23 \div d$

6. The minimum wage set in 1997 was $5.15 per hour. Evaluate the expression $40h$ where $h = \$5.15$ to find a worker's weekly salary.

   F $20.60   H $515.00

   G $200   J $206.00

7. What is the perimeter of a triangle with sides the following lengths: $2a + 4c$, $3c + 7$, and $6a - 4$. Simplify the expression.

   A $8a + 11c$

   B $6a + 7c + 3$

   C $8a + 7c + 3$

   D $8a + 7c + 11$

8. A hexagon is a 6-sided figure. Find the perimeter of a hexagon where all of the sides are the same length and the expression $x + y$ represents the length of a side. Simplify the expression.

   F $6x + 6y$

   G $6 + x + y$

   H $6x + y$

   J $6xy$

Problem Solving
Equations and Their Solutions

Write the correct answer.

1. The jet airplane was invented in 1939. This is 12 years after the first television was invented. Was television invented in 1927 or 1951?

   _____

2. There are three times as many students in the high school as in the junior high school, which has 330 students. Does the high school have 990 students or 110 students?

   _____

3. The frigate bird has been recorded at speeds up to 95 mi/h. The only faster bird ever recorded was the spine-tailed swift at 11 mi/h faster. Was the speed of the spine-tailed swift 84 mi/h or 106 mi/h?

   _____

4. As of 2004, there were 20.5 million Internet users in Canada. This is 6.6 million more Internet users than there were in Mexico. Were there 27.1 million or 13.9 million Internet users in Mexico?

   _____

Choose the letter for the best answer.

5. In the United States, the average school year is 180 days. This is 71 days less than the average school year in China. What is the average school year in China?

   A 251 days

   B 109 days

   C 151 days

   D 271 days

6. The longest suspension bridge in the world is the Akashi Kaikyo Bridge in Japan. Its main span is 1,290 feet longer than a mile. A mile is 5,280 feet. How long is the Akashi Kaikyo bridge?

   F 3,990 feet

   G 6,400 feet

   H 4,049 feet

   J 6,570 feet

7. *Ornithomimus* stood about 6 feet tall and was the fastest dinosaur at a speed of about 50 mi/h. The largest dinosaur, *Seismosaurus,* was 20 times as tall. How tall was *Seismosaurus?*

   A 12 feet

   B 70 feet

   C 120 feet

   D 26 feet

8. Milton collects sports trading cards. He has 80 baseball cards. He has half as many basketball cards as football cards. He has 20 more hockey cards than basketball cards and half as many football cards as baseball cards. How many hockey cards does he have?

   F 20 hockey cards

   G 40 hockey cards

   H 60 hockey cards

   J 80 hockey cards

LESSON 1-10

Problem Solving

Solving Equations by Adding or Subtracting

Write the correct answer.

1. In an online poll, 1,927 people voted for Coach as the best job at the Super Bowl. The job of Announcer received 8,055 more votes. Write and solve an equation to find how many votes the job of Announcer received.

   _____

2. In 2005, the largest bank in the world was UBS, Switzerland, with $1,533 billion in assets. This was $49 billion more than the largest bank in the United States, Citigroup. Write and solve an equation to find Citigroup's assets.

   _____

3. The two smallest countries in the world are Vatican City and Monaco. Vatican City is 1.37 square kilometers smaller than Monaco, which is 1.81 square kilometers in area. What is the area of Vatican City?

   _____

4. The Library of Congress is the largest library in the world. It has 29 million books, which is 10 million more than the National Library of Canada has. How many books does the National Library of Canada have?

   _____

Choose the letter for the best answer.

5. The first track on Sean's new CD has been playing for 55 seconds. This is 42 seconds less than the time of the entire first track. How long is the first track on this CD?

   A 37 seconds   C 97 seconds

   B 63 seconds   D 93 seconds

6. There are 45 students on the school football team. This is 13 more than the number of students on the basketball team. How many students are on the basketball team?

   F 58 students   H 32 students

   G 48 students   J 42 students

7. A used mountain bike costs $79.95. This is $120 less than the cost of a new one. If c is the cost of the new bike, which equation can you use to find the cost of a new bike?

   A $79.95 = c + 120$

   B $120 = 79.95 - c$

   C $79.95 = c - 120$

   D $120 = 79.95 + c$

8. The goal of the School Bake Sale is to raise $125 more than last year's sale. Last year the Bake Sale raised $320. If it reaches its goal, how much will the Bake Sale raise this year?

   F $445

   G $195

   H $525

   J $425

    Holt McDougal Mathematics

Problem Solving

LESSON 1-11

Solving Equations by Multiplying or Dividing

Write the correct answer.

1. The Panama Canal cost $387,000,000 to build. Each ship pays $34,000 to pass through the canal. How many ships had to pass through the canal to pay for the cost to build it?

2. The rate of exchange for currency changes daily. One day you could get $25 for 3,302.75 Japanese yen. Write and solve a multiplication equation to find the number of yen per dollar on that day.

3. Franklin D. Roosevelt was in office as president for 12 years. This is three times as long as Jimmy Carter was president. Write and solve an equation to show how long Jimmy Carter was president.

4. The mileage from Dallas to Miami is 1,332 miles. To the nearest hour, how many hours would it take to drive from Dallas to Miami at an average speed of 55 mi/h?

Choose the letter for the best answer.

5. The total bill for a bike rental for 8 hours was $38. How much per hour was the rental cost?

   A $8 per hour

   B $4.75 per hour

   C $30 per hour

   D $5.25 per hour

6. If a salesclerk earns $5.75 per hour, how many hours per week does she work to earn her weekly salary of $207?

   F 30 hours

   G 32 hours

   H 36 hours

   J 4 hours

7. At a cost of $0.07 per minute, which equation could you use to find out how many minutes you can talk for $3.15?

   A $0.07 \div m = 3.15

   B $3.15 \cdot m = 0.07

   C $0.07m = 3.15

   D $0.07 \div $3.15 = m$

8. Which equation shows how to find a runner's distance if he ran a total of m miles in 36 minutes at an average of a mile every 7.2 minutes?

   F $36 \div m = 7.2$

   G $7.2 \div m = 36$

   H $36m = 7.2$

   J $7.2 \div 36 = m$

Holt McDougal Mathematics

Problem Solving
LESSON 2-1

Integers

Write the correct answer.

1. The coldest place on record in the United States was in Alaska in 1971. It was 80 °F below zero. Write this temperature as an integer.

   _____

2. The temperature outside was –4 °F at Jared's house and –8 °F at Mario's house. Where was the temperature warmer?

   _____

3. A small business reported a net loss of $62,500 during its first year. In its second year, it reported a profit of $34,100. Write each amount as an integer.

   _____

4. For one day, Lacy recorded the low temperatures in five U.S. cities. The temperatures were 5 °C, –1° C, –3 °C, 2 °C, and 0 °C. Write the temperatures in order from least to greatest.

   _____

Choose the letter for the best answer.

5. Which number is not an integer?

   $-3; 5; \dfrac{1}{5}; 0$

   A –3   C $\dfrac{1}{5}$

   B 5   D 0

6. Basha says $\left|5\right|$ and $\left|-5\right|$ are the same number. Danny says $\left|5\right|$ and $\left|-5\right|$ are different numbers. Kim says $\left|5\right|$ and $\left|-5\right|$ both equal 0. Who is correct?

   F Basha
   G Danny
   H Kim
   J They are all wrong.

7. Use the table at right. Which continent has the highest point?

   A Asia   C Africa
   B South America D Australia

8. Use the table at right. Which continent has the lowest point?

   F Europe   G Australia
   H North America   J Asia

Continent	Highest Point (ft)	Lowest Point (ft)
North America	20,320	–282
South America	22,834	–131
Africa	19,340	–512
Asia	29,028	–1,339
Australia	7,310	–52
Europe	18,510	–92

Problem Solving

Adding Integers

Write the correct answer.

1. The temperature dropped 12 °F in 8 hours. If the final temperature was –7 °F, what was the starting temperature?

2. At 3 P.M., the temperature was 9 °F. By 11 P.M., it had dropped 31 °F. What was the temperature at 11 P.M.?

3. Tad owes John $23 and borrows $12 more. How much does Tad owe John now?

4. New Orleans, Louisiana, is 6 feet below sea level. The highest point in Louisiana, Driskill Mountain, is 541 feet higher than New Orleans. How high is Driskill Mountain?

5. A submarine submerged at a depth of –40 ft dives 57 ft more. What is the new depth of the submarine?

6. An airplane at 20,000 ft drops 2,500 ft in altitude. What is the new altitude?

Choose the letter for the best answer.

7. Last week, Jane made deposits of $64, $25, and $37 into her checking account. She then wrote checks for $52 and $49. What is the overall change in Jane's account balance?

   A –$99   C $126

   B $25   D $227

8. In Indianapolis, Indiana, the coldest recorded temperature was –23 °F. The hottest recorded temperature was 127 °F higher. What was the hottest temperature in Indianapolis?

   F 150 °F   H 104 °F

   G 127 °F   J –150 °F

9. Helena borrowed $189 from her parents to buy an electric bass. She paid back $56 last week and $64 this week. How much does Helena still owe her parents?

   A $133   C $69

   B $120   D $29

10. The Aral Sea and the Caspian Sea are actually lakes. The elevation of the Caspian Sea is 92 feet below sea level. The Aral Sea is 217 feet higher. What is the elevation of the Aral Sea?

   F –125 ft   H 309 ft

   G –309 ft   J 125 ft

LESSON
2-3

Problem Solving

Subtracting Integers

Write the correct answer.

1. The daytime temperature on Mercury can reach 430 °C. The nighttime temperature can drop to −180 °C. How much can the temperature drop during one day?

2. An ice cream company reported a net profit of $24,000 in 2002 and a net loss of $11,000 in 2003. How much did the company's profits change from 2002 to 2003?

3. A small business reported a net loss of $86,000 in 2004 and a net profit of $32,000 in 2005. How much did the company's profits change from 2004 to 2005?

4. The daytime high temperature on the Moon can reach 130 °C. At night, the temperature can drop to −110 °C. What is the difference between the high and low temperatures?

Choose the letter for the best answer.

5. The low point of the Tonga Trench, in the Pacific Ocean, is −10,630 meters. The low point of the Mariana Trench, also in the Pacific Ocean, is 890 meters lower. What is the depth of the Mariana Trench?

   A 10,630 meters

   B −11,520 meters

   C −9,740 meters

   D 9,740 meters

6. On Wednesday night in St. Petersburg, Russia, the temperature is −11°C. On the same night in Bombay, India, the temperature is 17°C. What is the difference in temperature?

   F −6 °C

   G 50 °C

   H −187 °C

   J 28 °C

7. Climax, Colorado, is the highest town in the United States at 11,560 feet. The lowest town is Calipatria, California, which is 185 feet below sea level. What is the difference in elevation?

   A −185 feet

   B 11,375 feet

   C 11,560 feet

   D 11,745 feet

8. The low point of the Japanese Trench, in the Pacific Ocean, is −10,372 meters. The low point of the Puerto Rico Trench, in the Atlantic Ocean, is 1,172 meters higher. What is the depth of the Puerto Rico Trench?

   F −9,200 meters

   G 8,200 meters

   H −1,172 meters

   J −11,544 meters

Holt McDougal Mathematics

LESSON 2-4

Problem Solving

Multiplying and Dividing Integers

Gerald recorded the temperature at 6-hour intervals for one 24-hour period. The chart shows his data.

Time	10:00 P.M.	4:00 A.M.	10:00 A.M.	4:00 P.M.	10:00 P.M.
Temperature (°F)	70	58	64	82	76

Write the correct answer.

1. If the temperature changed steadily, what was the change per hour from 10:00 P.M. the first day to 4:00 A.M.?

2. If the temperature changed steadily, what was the change per hour from 4:00 A.M. to 10:00 A.M.?

3. If the temperature changed steadily, what was the change per hour from 10:00 A.M. to 4:00 P.M.?

4. If the temperature changed steadily, what was the change per hour from 4:00 P.M. to 10:00 P.M. the second day?

Choose the letter for the best answer.

5. A small company had a profit of −$528 in January. If it continues to have the same profit each month for 4 months, what will be the company's total profit for 4 months?

   A   −$132
   B $132
   C   −$2,112
   D $2,112

6. Evi's watch is water resistant up to −15 feet. Mateo's watch is water resistant up to 8 times the depth of Evi's watch. Mateo's watch is water resistant to what maximum depth?

   F   −7 feet
   G   120 feet
   H   −120 feet
   J   7 feet

7. A submarine at −235 meters dives to a depth 8 times its initial depth. To what depth does the submarine dive?

   A   −227 meters
   B   −243 meters
   C   −1,880 meters
   D   −8,235 meters

8. A 1-kilogram rock dropped into the ocean would take 37 minutes to reach −6,660 meters. If the rock dropped steadily, how far would it fall in 1 minute?

   F   37 meters
   G   167 meters
   H   180 meters
   J   188 meters

Holt McDougal Mathematics

Problem Solving

LESSON 2-5

Solving Equations Containing Integers

Write the correct answer.

1. Jolene has 30 days to prepare for a bicycle race. She will bicycle 15 miles each day. How many miles will Jolene have bicycled during her training?

2. When the amount of money spent is greater than the amount of income, it is called a deficit. In 2002, the U.S. budget deficit was −$158 billion. By 2004, it was −$412 billion. How much did the deficit go up during those two years?

3. Two angles of a triangle have a sum of 110°. The sum of all three angles is 180°. What is the measure of the third angle?

4. The Statue of Liberty was erected in New York City in 1886. How old is the statue?

Choose the letter for the best answer.

5. Lonnie swam 3 miles each day for 45 days. How many miles did Lonnie swim?

   A 135 miles

   B 48 miles

   C 125 miles

   D 45 miles

6. On the hottest day in Richmond, Virginia, the temperature was 105 °F. On the coldest day, the temperature was 117 °F lower. What was the coldest temperature in Richmond?

   F −117 °F

   G −12 °F

   H 12 °F

   J 117 °F

7. Mr. Marco sold 50 shares of Gizmo stock for $1,250. What was the selling price of the stock per share?

   A $1,200

   B $250

   C $50

   D $25

8. The U.S. Bullion Depository at Fort Knox contains about 147 million troy ounces of gold. At a market price of $400 per troy ounce, what is the approximate value of the gold stored at Fort Knox?

   F $6 billion

   G $60 billion

   H $560 million

   J $560 billion

Holt McDougal Mathematics

LESSON 2-6

Problem Solving
Prime Factorization

Write the correct answer.

1. The width of a swimming pool (in feet) is a prime number greater than 10. The width and length of the pool are factors of 408. What are the dimensions of the pool?

2. The area of the dining room at Thomas Jefferson's home in Monticello is about 342 square feet. If the approximate length of one side is a prime number less than 25, what are the approximate dimensions of the room?

3. A university has a lounge that can be converted into a meeting hall for 250 people. If the hall is filled and everyone is in equal groups, what are the different ways the people can be grouped so that there are no more than 10 groups?

4. You want to read a mystery that has 435 pages. If you read the same number of pages per day and the number is a prime number greater than 20, how many pages per day will you read?

Choose the letter of the best answer.

5. There are 228 seventh graders. Each seventh-grade homeroom starts the year with the same number of students and has at least 15 students. What is the least number of rooms that are needed?

   A 17
   B 19
   C 12
   D 21

6. Solve this riddle: I am a number whose prime factors are all the prime numbers between 6 and 15. No factor is repeated. What number am I?

   F 9,009
   G 91
   H 1,001
   J 6,006

7. What is the prime factorization of 1,485?

   A $3 \cdot 3 \cdot 3 \cdot 5 \cdot 11$
   B $3 \cdot 3 \cdot 5 \cdot 5 \cdot 11$
   C $3 \cdot 5 \cdot 9 \cdot 11$
   D $5 \cdot 11 \cdot 27$

8. Solve this riddle: I am a prime factor of 39 and 65. What number am I?

   F 3
   G 5
   H 11
   J 13

Holt McDougal Mathematics

LESSON
2-7

Problem Solving

Greatest Common Factor

Write the correct answer.

1. Fabric is sold in stores from bolts that are 45 or 60 inches wide. What is the width of the widest strips of fabric you can cut from either bolt without wasting any of the fabric if each strip has the same width?

2. The parents are making sandwiches for the class picnic. They have 72 turkey slices, 48 cheese slices, and 96 tomato slices. What is the greatest number of sandwiches they can make if each sandwich has the same filling?

3. Two bicycle enthusiasts are leaving Cincinnati at the same time. One is biking 840 miles to Boston. The other is biking 440 miles to Atlanta. What is the greatest number of miles a day each can bike if they want to cover equal distances each day?

4. A fruit salad made on a TV cooking program requires chunks of cantaloupe and honeydew. What is the greatest number of servings you can make using all of the fruit if you have 30 chunks of cantaloupe and 42 chunks of honeydew?

Choose the letter for the best answer.

5. Ari is making patriotic pins. He has 105 red ribbons, 147 white ribbons, and 189 blue ribbons. What is the greatest number of identical pins he can make if he uses all his ribbons?

   A 52 pins   C 93 pins

   B 19 pins   D 21 pins

6. Cheryce is making fruit baskets. She has 60 bananas, 72 pears, 96 apples, and 108 oranges. What is the greatest number of equal baskets she can make with the fruit?

   F 3 baskets   H 12 baskets

   G 6 baskets   J 24 baskets

7. There are 100 senators and 435 representatives in the United States Congress. How many identical groups could be formed from all the senators and representatives?

   A 1 group

   B 5 groups

   C 10 groups

   D 15 groups

8. There are 14 baseball teams in the American League and 16 teams in the National League. There are 30 National Hockey League teams. If equal groups of teams are formed, how many hockey teams will be in each group?

   F 3 hockey teams

   G 8 hockey teams

   H 7 hockey teams

   J 15 hockey teams

     Holt McDougal Mathematics

Problem Solving

Least Common Multiple

Write the correct answer.

1. Earth revolves around the sun every year. Jupiter revolves around the sun every 12 years. If Earth and Jupiter passed the same point of the sun sometime in 2002, when will they pass that point together again?

2. House representatives are elected every 2 years. The President of the United States is elected every 4 years. Both will be elected in 2008. When is the next year after 2008 both will be elected?

3. A cat runs a mile every 2 minutes. A squirrel runs a mile every 5 minutes. A cat and a squirrel start together running around a 1-mile track. How long will it be before they meet at the starting point?

4. A car manual recommends changing the oil every 5,000 miles and inspecting the engine coolant system every 15,000 miles. At how many miles will both be done together for the first time? for the second time?

Choose the letter for the best answer.

5. Mr. Walters receives a dividend every 5 months and a royalty payment every 6 months. He received both in January 2006. When is the next time he would receive both payments in the same month?

   A January 2007

   B April 2008

   C July 2006

   D July 2008

6. Rag Rite Cloth Store always rounds amounts less than whole yards up to the next yard for ribbon purchases. The ribbon that you want to buy comes in rolls of 8 feet. How many rolls should you buy to get the best buy? (Hint: 1 yard = 3 feet)

   F 1 roll

   G 2 rolls

   H 3 rolls

   J 4 rolls

7. The sanitation department picks up recyclable plastics every 3 days. The paper recycling center picks up papers every 4 days. They both picked up on May 4. When will they next pick up on the same day?

   A May 7

   B May 12

   C May 11

   D May 16

8. Hal and Jess both volunteer at the local nursing home. Hal volunteers every 6 days, and Jess volunteers every 8 days. They were both there on Monday. In how many days will they both volunteer together again?

   F in 14 days

   G in 24 days

   H in 48 days

   J in 2 days

Holt McDougal Mathematics

LESSON 2-9	**Problem Solving**
	Equivalent Fractions and Mixed Numbers

Write the correct answer.

1. Bert bicycles 136 miles each week. If he bikes the same distance daily and bikes each day of the week, how many miles does he bike each day? Write your answer as a mixed number.

2. The Eiffel Tower in Paris, France, was designed so well that even in the highest winds the tower never sways more than $4\frac{1}{2}$ inches. Write two fractions that are equivalent to $4\frac{1}{2}$.

3. In October 2000, almost 13 inches of rain fell in Miami, Florida, in a 24-hour period. Write a fraction that shows about how many $\frac{1}{4}$ inches of rain fell on that one day.

4. Elena is 58 inches tall. Write a mixed number to represent her height in feet.

Choose the letter for the best answer.

5. Randi runs 48 miles each week. She runs the same distance daily and runs each day of the week. How many miles does she run each day? Write your answer as a mixed number.

   A $6\frac{6}{7}$ miles   C $6\frac{7}{48}$ miles

   B $6\frac{5}{6}$ miles   D $7\frac{1}{7}$ miles

6. A bakery used $4\frac{3}{4}$ cups of salt to make 120 loaves of sourdough bread. Write a fraction that shows how many $\frac{1}{4}$ cups of salt were used to make the bread.

   F $\frac{30}{4}$ cups   H $\frac{12}{4}$ cups

   G $\frac{24}{4}$ cups   J $\frac{19}{4}$ cups

7. One of the driest summers in the Northeast was in 1909, with $\frac{896}{100}$ inches of precipitation. Which mixed number is equivalent to $\frac{896}{100}$?

   A $89\frac{6}{10}$ C $8\frac{24}{25}$

   B $8\frac{96}{10}$ D $8\frac{4}{5}$

8. The Central Ohio Transit Authority has $957\frac{3}{5}$ miles of routes. Which fraction is equivalent to $957\frac{3}{5}$?

   F $\frac{4,781}{5}$ H $\frac{4,783}{5}$

   G $\frac{4,788}{5}$ J $\frac{9,573}{5}$

Holt McDougal Mathematics

Problem Solving

LESSON 2-10

Equivalent Fractions and Decimals

Write the correct answer.

1. On a test, Shane answered 37 out of 40 questions correctly. What portion of his answers was correct? Write your answer as a decimal rounded to the nearest thousandth.

   _____

2. Sammy Sosa hit 66 home runs in 1998. He had 643 at bats. Write his home run average as a decimal rounded to the nearest thousandth.

   _____

3. In February, Chicago receives an average of $1\frac{2}{5}$ inches of rain. Write a decimal to show the number of inches of rain.

   _____

4. On a test, Ellen answered 51 out of 64 questions correctly. What portion of her answers was correct? Write your answer as a decimal rounded to the nearest thousandth.

   _____

Choose the letter for the best answer.

Use the graph for 5–6.

5. Which mixed number shows the energy, in quadrillions of BTU, consumed in Eastern Europe in 2003?

   A 53

   B $53\frac{1}{4}$

   C $53\frac{1}{2}$

   D $53\frac{4}{5}$

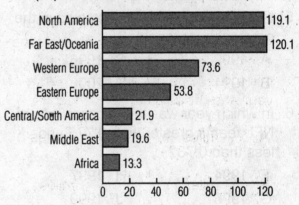

World Energy Consumption 2003
(in quadrillions of British Thermal Units, BTU)

North America	119.1
Far East/Oceania	120.1
Western Europe	73.6
Eastern Europe	53.8
Central/South America	21.9
Middle East	19.6
Africa	13.3

0 20 40 60 80 100 120

6. Which mixed number shows the energy, in quadrillions of BTU, consumed in the Middle East in 2003?

   F $19\frac{1}{10}$

   G $19\frac{2}{5}$

   H $19\frac{3}{5}$

   J $19\frac{3}{10}$

7. Jill sold 478 out of 520 tickets to the opening night of her theater performance. What portion of the tickets did she sell?

   A 0.998

   B 1.088

   C 0.919

   D 0.081

8. The high school sold 369 out of 460 tickets to the opening night of a concert series. What portion of the tickets was sold?

   F 0.198

   G 0.829

   H 1.247

   J 0.802

Holt McDougal Mathematics

Problem Solving

LESSON 2-11

Comparing and Ordering Rational Numbers

Write the correct answer.

1. Some of the wettest summers in the Northeast had the following amounts of precipitation, in inches: $14\frac{7}{10}$, $14\frac{1}{4}$, $14\frac{4}{5}$, and 14.69. Order the amounts of precipitation from least to greatest.

_____

_____

2. The U.S. soybean crop decreased each year from 2001 to 2003. Production for each year was approximately $2\frac{3}{4}$, 2.9, $2\frac{2}{5}$ billion bushels. Match the soybean crop, in billions of bushels, with its year.

_____

_____

3. Mark's batting average last year was 0.334. Ken's was 0.304, and Ty's was 0.343. Write the batting averages in order from lowest to highest.

_____

_____

4. Kiki lives 0.097 miles from the school, and George lives 0.131 miles from the school. Who lives farthest from the school?

_____

_____

Choose the letter for the best answer. Use the graph for problems 5–6.

5. In which year did NFL teams have the greatest success rate?

  A 1992   C 1996

  B 1994   D 2000

6. In which year was the success rate of NFL teams greater than 0.775 and less than 0.78?

  F 1994   H 1997

  G 1995   J 1999

NFL Field Goal Success Rate

Year	Rate
1992	0.726
1993	0.766
1994	0.789
1995	0.774
1996	0.800
1997	0.781
1998	0.796
1999	0.777
2000	0.797

       Holt McDougal Mathematics

LESSON	**Problem Solving**
3-1	***Estimating with Decimals***

Write the correct answer.

1. The Spanish Club makes a profit of $1.85 on every pie sold at a bake sale. The goal is to earn $40.00 selling pies. Will the club have to sell more than or fewer than 20 pies to meet the goal?

_____

2. Murray and 4 friends split the cost of a pizza, with each paying the same amount. Murray has $3.36. The pizza costs $14.20. Does Murray have enough to pay for his share? About how much is his share?

_____

3. Luis has 22 MB of free space on his MP3 player. He wants to download 5 songs. They will take up 5.1, 4.1, 4.3, 8.2, and 3.6 MB of space. Does Luis have enough free space? About how much space is needed?

_____

4. Debi has a gift certificate worth $50 for a local book-and-music store. She decides to buy a book that costs $18.95 and some CDs. Each CD costs $13.99. How many CDs can she buy?

_____

Choose the letter for the best answer.

This table shows the number of dollars foreign tourists spent while visiting different countries in 2003.

Spending by Tourists in 2003

Country	Amount Spent by Foreign Tourists ($ billions)
United States	65.1
Spain	41.7
France	36.3
Italy	31.3
Germany	22.8
United Kingdom	19.5
China	17.4
Austria	13.6
Turkey	13.2
Greece	10.6
Mexico	9.5

5. The amount spent in which two countries was about equal to the amount spent in Italy?

  A Austria and Turkey

  B United Kingdom and China

  C Germany and Greece

  D Austria and China

6. About how much did tourists spend in Spain, France, and Italy all together?

  F $111 billion   H $78 billion

  G $109 billion   J $67 billion

7. If the amount spent by foreign tourists remains the same, about how much will foreign tourists spend in the United States over 5 years?

  F $120 billion   H $350 billion

  G $250 billion   J $450 billion

LESSON
3-2

Problem Solving
Adding and Subtracting Decimals

Write the correct answer.

1. In the Pacific Ocean, the Philippine Trench is 10.05 kilometers deep. In the Atlantic Ocean, the Brazil Basin is 6.12 kilometers deep. How much deeper is the Philippine Trench than the Brazil Basin?

_____

2. Hawaii's Mauna Kea measures 9.75 kilometers from its base to its peak. The base of Mauna Kea lies 5.55 kilometers below the ocean. What is the height of the part of Mauna Kea that is above sea level?

_____

3. A team of mountain climbers makes camp 1.48 kilometers above sea level. They climb another 2.91 kilometers to the mountain's peak. How tall is the mountain?

_____

4. At dawn, the temperature at the summit of a mountain was –8.5 °C. By noon, the temperature had increased 3.6 °C. What was the temperature at noon?

_____

Choose the letter for the best answer.

This table gives the heights of the tallest mountains on each of the seven continents.

The Seven Summits

Mountain	Country	Height (km)
Mt. Everest	Nepal-Tibet	8.85
Mt. Aconcagua	Argentina	6.96
Mt. McKinley	United States	6.19
Mt. Kilimanjaro	Tanzania	5.90
Mt. Elbrus	Russia	5.64
Vinson Massif	Antarctica	4.90
Puncak Jaya	New Guinea	4.88

5. In 2000, Joby Ogwyn became the youngest person to climb each of the seven summits. How much higher did he climb on Vinson Massif than on Puncak Jaya?

  A 0.02 km   C 0.18 km

  B 0.12 km   D 9.78 km

6. Mt. Kilimanjaro, Mt. Elbrus, and Mt. Aconcagua were the first three of the seven summits Joby climbed. What was the total height he climbed?

  F 16.2 km   H 18.5 km

  G 17.5 km   J 22 km

7. Mt. Aconcagua is about 1.3 kilometers taller than which mountain?

  A Mt. Everest

  B Mt. Elbrus

  C Mt. McKinley

  D Vinson Massif

     Holt McDougal Mathematics

LESSON 3-3 — Problem Solving

Multiplying Decimals

Write the correct answer.

1. A group of 6 adults bought tickets to a play at the community center. The tickets cost $17.50 each. How much did the tickets cost in all?

_____

2. Student tickets for the basketball playoffs cost $9.25 each. How much do 9 student tickets cost?

_____

3. Movie tickets for senior citizens cost 0.8 times as much as regular adult tickets. Adult tickets cost $7.50. How much do senior citizen tickets cost?

_____

4. About 30.5 million Americans attend classical music concerts. The average concertgoer attends 2.9 concerts per year. About how many tickets to classical concerts are sold each year?

_____

Choose the letter for the best answer.

5. The population of Illinois in 2000 was about 1.57 times its population in 1940. If the population of Illinois in 1940 was about 7.9 million, what was its population in 2000, to the nearest tenth of a million?

  A 1.2 million

  B 9.5 million

  C 12.4 million

  D 15.8 million

6. In 2004, the United States had 32.5 million broadband subscribers. This number is expected to increase 1.75 times by 2008. How many broadband subscribers is the United States expected to have in 2008?

  F 24.375 million

  G 34.25 million

  H 56.875 million

  J 568.75 million

7. Nauru and Gibraltar are among the smallest countries in the world. Nauru has about 3.28 times the area that Gibraltar does. Gibraltar is 2.5 square miles. What is the area of Nauru?

  A 0.78 mi^2

  B 0.82 mi^2

  C 5.78 mi^2

  D 8.2 mi^2

8. From 1999 to 2008, the United States Mint is issuing a series of 50 quarters representing each of the 50 states. What is the cost of collecting 10 of each quarter?

  F $100

  G $125

  H $150

  J $250

Holt McDougal Mathematics

LESSON	**Problem Solving**
3-4	*Dividing Decimals*

Write the correct answer.

1. Fran has a plank of wood 4.65 meters long. She wants to cut it into pieces 0.85 meters long. How many pieces of wood that length can she cut from the plank?

2. Jeremy has a box of 500 nails that weighs 1.35 kilograms. He uses 60 nails to build a birdhouse. How much do the nails in the birdhouse weigh?

3. Rhosanda is downloading a file from the Internet. The size of the file is 7.45 MB. The file is downloading at the rate of 0.095 MB per second. How many seconds will it take to download the entire file? Round your answer to the nearest second.

4. Sean has a piece of poster board with an area of 476.28 square centimeters. He cuts it into equal-sized squares, each with an area of 39.69 square centimeters. How many squares can he cut from the piece of poster board?

Choose the letter for the best answer.

5. Mount McKinley, in Alaska, is about 3.848 miles high. If a mountain climber can climb 0.25 miles per day, about how long, to the nearest day, would it take to climb Mount McKinley?

   A about 5 days

   B about 8 days

   C about 12 days

   D about 15 days

6. In 2000, a production worker in Japan who worked 38.5 hours in a week would have earned an average of $847. What was the hourly wage?

   F $2.20 per hour

   G $3.20 per hour

   H $22.00 per hour

   J $32.00 per hour

7. In the 2000 Summer Olympics, Michael Johnson ran the 400-meter race in 43.84 seconds. To the nearest hundredth, what was his speed in meters per second?

   A 9.12 meters per second

   B 10.96 meters per second

   C 1.09 meters per second

   D 91.24 meters per second

8. In the 2000 Summer Olympics, the United States relay team ran the 1,600-meter relay in 2 minutes, 56.35 seconds. To the nearest hundredth, what was the speed for the relay race in meters per second?

   F 2.83 meters per second

   G 6.24 meters per second

   H 9.07 meters per second

   J 28.39 meters per second

Holt McDougal Mathematics

Problem Solving

LESSON 3-5

Solving Equations Containing Decimals

Write the correct answer.

1. The diameter of the secondary mirror in NASA's Hubble telescope is 0.3 meter. The primary mirror is 8 times as large. What is the diameter of the primary mirror?

2. A cubic centimeter of titanium weighs 4.507 grams. The same volume of gold weighs 19.3 grams. How much more does a cubic centimeter of gold weigh?

3. Brianna drives 3.35 miles to work every day. This is 1.75 miles less than Darius drives to work every day. How far does Darius drive to work?

4. The weight of an object on Mars is 0.38 times its weight on Earth. How much would a 125-pound person weigh on Mars?

Choose the letter for the best answer.

The table shows the orbital velocity of some of the planets.

5. How much greater is the orbital velocity of Mercury than that of Uranus?

   A 33.97 miles per second

   B 25.51 miles per second

   C 7.03 miles per second

   D 4.23 miles per second

6. How many miles does Mercury travel in an hour?

   F 1,784.4 miles

   G 107,064 miles

   H 10,706.4 miles

   J 17,844 miles

7. How many miles does Jupiter travel in a minute?

   A 8.12 miles

   B 81.2 miles

   C 48.72 miles

   D 487.2 miles

Planets' Orbital Velocity

Planet	Orbital Velocity (mi/s)
Mercury	29.74
Venus	21.76
Earth	18.5
Mars	14.99
Jupiter	8.12
Saturn	6.02
Uranus	4.23

8. During the time it takes Saturn to travel 32,508 miles, how much time has elapsed on Earth?

   F 5,400 minutes

   G 1,757.19 minutes

   H 195,698 seconds

   J 90 minutes

Holt McDougal Mathematics

LESSON 3-6

Problem Solving
Estimating with Fractions

Write the correct answer.

1. At the beach, Richard rides the waves on a boogie board that is $3\frac{2}{3}$ feet long. Laura rides a $7\frac{1}{2}$-foot surfboard. Estimate the difference in length of the 2 boards.

_____

2. Jorgé had $5\frac{1}{3}$ jugs of apple cider. He used $2\frac{5}{6}$ jugs for a party. About how much apple cider does he have left?

3. Sari jogs $2\frac{3}{4}$ miles on Monday, $3\frac{5}{6}$ miles on Wednesday, and $2\frac{1}{3}$ miles on Friday. Estimate her total distance for the week.

_____

4. Robert's hand is $2\frac{7}{8}$ inches wide. When Robert uses his hand to estimate the width of his desk, he finds that the desk is about $11\frac{3}{4}$ hands wide. About how many inches wide is the desk?

_____

Choose the letter for the best answer.

This table shows the total amount of snow to fall in 5 cities during 2003.

Snowfall During 2003

City	Amount of Snow (in.)
Chicago, IL	$17\frac{2}{5}$
Indianapolis, IN	$44\frac{1}{10}$
Marquette, MI	$191\frac{4}{5}$
Moline, IL	$23\frac{4}{5}$
Providence, RI	$58\frac{9}{10}$

5. About how much snow all together fell in the two cities in Illinois?
   A 40 inches   C 44 inches
   B 41 inches   D 61 inches

6. About how much more snow fell in Providence than in Indianapolis?
   F 35 inches   H 15 inches
   G 20 inches   J 10 inches

7. Which city had about 11 times as much snow as Chicago?
   A Indianapolis   C Moline
   B Marquette   D Providence

8. About how much more snow fell in Indianapolis than in Moline?
   F 20 inches   H 24 inches
   G 22 inches   J 30 inches

Holt McDougal Mathematics

LESSON 3-7

Problem Solving

Adding and Subtracting Fractions

Write the correct answer.

1. During the recycling drive, $\frac{1}{5}$ of the material collected was bottles and $\frac{1}{4}$ was paper. Cardboard boxes made up $\frac{1}{10}$ of the material. How much of the total do these three items represent?

_____

2. Decorations for school dances take $\frac{1}{5}$ of the student council's budget. Entertainment takes $\frac{3}{10}$ of the budget. What fraction of the budget is left?

_____

3. The school environmental club made a poster to celebrate Earth Day. The poster is $\frac{7}{8}$ yard long and $\frac{2}{3}$ yard wide. What is the difference in the length and width of the poster?

_____

4. Three students ran for president of the student council. Eddie received $\frac{1}{5}$ of the votes. Tamara received $\frac{3}{8}$ of the votes. Levi received the rest. Which student won the election?

_____

Choose the letter for the best answer.

5. The Reeds budget $\frac{1}{3}$ of their income for rent and $\frac{1}{4}$ for food. How much of their budget is left?

A $\frac{1}{2}$

B $\frac{3}{4}$

C $\frac{5}{12}$

D $\frac{7}{12}$

6. Jasmine's CD collection is $\frac{3}{8}$ jazz, $\frac{1}{4}$ rap, and the rest rock music. What fraction of her CDs is rock music?

F $\frac{1}{4}$

G $\frac{3}{8}$

H $\frac{1}{2}$

J $\frac{5}{8}$

7. Wong has 2 boxes of saltwater taffy. One box contains $\frac{3}{4}$ pound, and the other box contains $\frac{7}{10}$ pound. How much taffy does he have all together?

A $\frac{9}{10}$ pound

B $1\frac{9}{20}$ pounds

C $1\frac{1}{2}$ pounds

D $1\frac{13}{20}$ pounds

8. In 1992, about $\frac{43}{100}$ people voted for Bill Clinton for President. About $\frac{1}{5}$ voted for Ross Perot and the rest voted for George Bush. About how many voted for George Bush?

F about $\frac{37}{100}$

G about $\frac{52}{100}$

H about $\frac{57}{100}$

J about $\frac{3}{5}$

Holt McDougal Mathematics

LESSON
3-8

Problem Solving
Adding and Subtracting Mixed Numbers

Write the correct answer.

1. A female gray whale is $45\frac{1}{4}$ feet long. A male gray whale is $43\frac{1}{2}$ feet long. How much longer is the female than the male gray whale?

   _____

2. At birth, a pilot whale is $4\frac{3}{5}$ feet long. A newborn gray whale is $15\frac{1}{4}$ feet long. How much longer is the newborn gray whale?

   _____

3. A manatee weighs $\frac{1}{2}$ ton. A walrus weighs $1\frac{3}{4}$ tons. A narwhal weighs $1\frac{1}{2}$ tons. What is the total weight of all 3 animals?

   _____

4. A bottle-nosed dolphin can leap $15\frac{1}{8}$ feet out of the water. The world record high jump for a human is $8\frac{1}{24}$ feet. How much higher can a dolphin leap than a human?

   _____

Choose the letter for the best answer.

5. At a wildlife park, the killer whale show lasts $\frac{5}{8}$ of an hour. The guided tour of the park takes $2\frac{1}{2}$ hours. How long will it take to do both activities?

   A $3\frac{1}{8}$ hours C $3\frac{5}{8}$ hours

   B $2\frac{5}{8}$ hours D $1\frac{7}{8}$ hours

6. Jeremy walks $3\frac{1}{2}$ miles while visiting a wildlife park. Shawna hikes a $4\frac{3}{8}$-mile long nature trail. How much farther does Shawna walk?

   F $\frac{3}{8}$ of a mile H $\frac{7}{8}$ of a mile

   G $\frac{5}{8}$ of a mile J $1\frac{1}{8}$ of a mile

7. Dog food comes in $5\frac{7}{8}$-pound bags and $12\frac{3}{4}$-pound bags. Find the total weight of 2 small and 1 large bags.

   A $22\frac{7}{8}$ pounds C $24\frac{1}{2}$ pounds

   B $23\frac{1}{2}$ pounds D $25\frac{3}{4}$ pounds

8. A movie lasts $2\frac{1}{6}$ hours. A baseball game lasts $3\frac{2}{3}$ hours. How much longer does the game last?

   F $\frac{5}{6}$ hours H $1\frac{1}{3}$ hours

   G $1\frac{1}{6}$ hours J $1\frac{1}{2}$ hours

Problem Solving

LESSON 3-9

Multiplying Fractions and Mixed Numbers

Write the correct answer.

1. Ariel's English homework is to read 24 pages. She reads $\frac{1}{8}$ of the assignment on the bus ride home. How many pages does she read on the bus?

2. When a group of 40 friends goes to the movies at a multiplex, $\frac{1}{5}$ of the group decides to watch a science fiction movie. How many of the group see the science fiction movie?

3. As of 1990, the American Indian population was about 2,000,000. About $\frac{1}{5}$ were Cherokee. About how many members of the Cherokee tribe were there in 1990?

4. Ron spends 3 hours painting a picture. Ashley spends $2\frac{2}{3}$ as long creating a sculpture. How long does Ashley work on her sculpture?

Choose the letter for the best answer.

5. One cup of dry dog food weighs $1\frac{4}{5}$ ounces. A K9 dog eats $6\frac{1}{3}$ cups of food a day. How many ounces of food does the dog eat each day?

   A $4\frac{8}{15}$ ounces   C $11\frac{2}{5}$ ounces

   B $8\frac{2}{15}$ ounces   D $3\frac{14}{27}$ ounces

6. Max has enough chicken to make $8\frac{1}{2}$ servings of salad. He needs $\frac{1}{8}$ pound of chicken per serving. How much chicken does he have?

   F 8 pounds   H $8\frac{5}{8}$ pounds

   G $1\frac{1}{16}$ pounds   J $2\frac{1}{2}$ pounds

7. A meteorite found in Willamette, Oregon, weighed $\frac{7}{10}$ as much as one found in Armanti, Western Mongolia. The meteorite found in Armanti weighed 22 tons. How much did the one in Oregon weigh?

   A $31\frac{1}{5}$ tons   C $22\frac{7}{10}$ tons

   B $21\frac{3}{10}$ tons   D $15\frac{2}{5}$ tons

8. Nicole takes part in a $12\frac{1}{2}$-mile walk-a-thon to raise money for charity. She stops $\frac{1}{2}$ of the way to rest. How much farther must Nicole walk to finish the walk-a-thon?

   F $6\frac{1}{4}$ miles   H 12 miles

   G $6\frac{1}{2}$ miles   J 25 miles

Holt McDougal Mathematics

Problem Solving

LESSON 3-10

Dividing Fractions and Mixed Numbers

Write the correct answer.

1. The Wheeling Bridge in West Virginia is about $307\frac{4}{5}$ meters long. If you walk with a stride of about $\frac{3}{10}$ meter, how many steps would it take you to cross this suspension bridge?

2. The Flathead Rail Tunnel in Montana is about $7\frac{3}{4}$ miles long. If a train travels through the tunnel at a speed of about $1\frac{1}{2}$ miles per minute, how long will it take to pass from one end of the tunnel to the other?

3. A hiking trail is $6\frac{2}{3}$ miles long. It has 4 exercise stations, spaced evenly along the trail. What is the distance between each exercise station?

4. Jamal buys a strip of 25 postage stamps. The strip of stamps is $21\frac{7}{8}$ inches long. How long is each stamp?

Choose the letter for the best answer.

5. Matt wants to decorate his skateboard with decals. His skateboard is $28\frac{3}{4}$ inches long. The decals are $5\frac{1}{2}$ inches long. If Matt arranges them in a line from the front to the back, how many decals will fit?

   A 5 decals   C 7 decals

   B 6 decals   D 8 decals

6. A square floor tile measures $\frac{3}{4}$ square feet. How many tiles are required to cover a 200 square foot floor?

   F 150 tiles   H 275 tiles

   G 267 tiles   J 300 tiles

7. Bev buys a sleeve of ball bearings for her skateboard. Each of the bearings is $1\frac{1}{5}$ inches wide. The sleeve is $9\frac{3}{5}$ inches long. How many bearings are in the sleeve?

   A 5 bearings   C 9 bearings

   B 8 bearings   D 12 bearings

8. The average hamster weighs about $\frac{1}{4}$ pound. The total weight of all the hamsters in a cage in a pet store is $1\frac{1}{2}$ pounds. How many hamsters are in the cage?

   F 3 hamsters   H 5 hamsters

   G 4 hamsters   J 6 hamsters

LESSON 3-11

Problem Solving

Solving Equations Containing Fractions

Write the correct answer.

1. At the 2002 Winter Olympics, Austria won 2 gold medals. This was $\frac{1}{8}$ of the total medals Austria won. How many medals did Austria win?

_____

2. At the 2002 Winter Olympics, Germany won 35 medals, of which 16 were silver. They won $1\frac{1}{3}$ times as many silver medals as gold medals. How many gold medals did Germany win?

_____

3. Jesse plays ice hockey. He is on the ice $\frac{2}{5}$ of each game. A game lasts 45 minutes, divided into 3 periods. How many minutes is Jesse on the ice during each game?

_____

4. Amelia's soccer team won $\frac{3}{4}$ of its games. The team won 18 games. How many games did the team play?

_____

Choose the letter for the best answer.

5. At the 2002 Winter Olympics, China won 8 medals. The United States won $4\frac{1}{4}$ times as many medals as China did. How many medals did the United States win?

   A 24 medals   C 34 medals

   B 32 medals   D 40 medals

6. Juanita's water bottle contains $1\frac{7}{8}$ liters. She uses her bottle to fill Felix's. When she is done, her bottle contains $\frac{1}{4}$ liter. How many liters can Felix's bottle hold?

   F $\frac{7}{8}$ liter   H $1\frac{5}{8}$ liters

   G $1\frac{1}{8}$ liters   J $2\frac{1}{8}$ liters

7. Yoriko ran $6\frac{1}{2}$ laps of the track. Each lap is $\frac{1}{4}$ of a mile. How many miles did she run?

   A $6\frac{5}{8}$ miles   C 2 miles

   B $4\frac{1}{2}$ miles   D $1\frac{5}{8}$ miles

8. Rocky runs $3\frac{1}{2}$ miles each week. Leroy runs $5\frac{1}{3}$ miles each week. How much farther does Leroy run?

   F $1\frac{1}{2}$ miles   H $2\frac{1}{6}$ miles

   G $1\frac{5}{6}$ miles   J $2\frac{1}{4}$ miles

    Holt McDougal Mathematics

Problem Solving
Ratios

Write the correct answer.

1. The Rockport Diner has 8 seats at the counter and 32 seats at tables. Of these seats, 16 are taken. Write the ratio of seats taken to empty seats in simplest form three ways.

2. During the 2001 WNBA season, the Los Angeles Sparks had 28 wins and only 4 losses. Write the ratio of wins to games played in simplest form three ways.

3. For every 300 people surveyed in 2002, 186 said their favorite Winter Olympic sport was figure skating. Write this ratio in simplest form three ways.

4. In 2004, George W. Bush received 286 electoral votes, and John Kerry received 251, and 1 elector voted for John Edwards. Write the ratio of Bush's electoral votes to total electoral votes in simplest form three ways.

Choose the letter for the best answer.

5. There are 62 girls in the seventh grade and 58 boys in the eighth grade. Each grade has 120 students. Which statement correctly compares the ratios of boys to girls in each grade?

   A The eighth-grade ratio is greater.

   B The seventh-grade ratio is greater.

   C The eighth-grade ratio is lesser.

   D Both ratios are equal.

6. Matt has 6 video racing games and 8 video sports games. Which ratio is the ratio of racing games to total video games in simplest form?

   F $\dfrac{3}{4}$ H $\dfrac{4}{3}$

   G $\dfrac{3}{7}$ J $\dfrac{4}{7}$

7. Which player has the greatest ratio of baskets to total shots?

   A Marisol

   B Nina

   C Joanne

   D Talia

	Baskets	Missed Shots
Marisol	8	8
Nina	7	5
Joanne	2	4
Talia	5	3

Holt McDougal Mathematics

Problem Solving

Rates

Write the correct answer.

1. A truck driver drives from Cincinnati to Boston in 14 hours. The distance traveled is 840 miles. What is the truck driver's average rate of speed?

2. Melanie earns $97.50 in 6 hours. Earl earns $296.00 in 20 hours. Who earns a higher rate of pay per hour?

3. Mr. Tanney buys a 10-trip train ticket for $82.50. Ms. Elmer buys an unlimited weekly pass for $100 and uses it for 12 trips during the week. Write the unit cost per trip for each person.

4. Metropolitan Middle School has 564 students and 24 teachers. Eastern Middle School has 623 students and 28 teachers. Which school has the lower unit rate of students per teacher?

Choose the letter for the best answer.

5. Which shows 20 pounds per 5 gallons as a unit rate?

   A $\dfrac{20\ lb}{1\ gal}$ C $\dfrac{5\ lb}{1\ gal}$

   B $\dfrac{4\ lb}{1\ gal}$ D $\dfrac{1\ gal}{4\ lb}$

6. What is the unit price of a 6-ounce tube of toothpaste that costs $3.75?

   F $0.06
   G $0.23
   H $0.62
   J $0.63

7. Max bought 16 gallons of gas for $40.64. Lydia bought 12 gallons of gas for $31.08. Kesia bought 18 gallons of gas for $45.72. Who got the best buy?

   A Max got the best buy.

   B Lydia got the best buy.

   C Lydia and Kesia both paid the same rate, which is better than Max's rate.

   D Max and Kesia both paid the same rate, which is better than Lydia's rate.

8. A pack of 12 8-ounce bottles of water costs $3.36. What is the unit cost per ounce of bottled water?

   F $0.03 per ounce
   G $0.04 per ounce
   H $0.28 per bottle
   J $0.42 per bottle

Holt McDougal Mathematics

Problem Solving
Identifying and Writing Proportions

Write the correct answer.

1. Jeremy earns $234 for 36 hours of work. Miguel earns $288 for 40 hours of work. Are the pay rates of these two people proportional? Explain.

2. Marnie bought two picture frames. One is 5 inches by 8 inches. The other is 15 inches by 24 inches. Are the ratios of length to width proportional for these frames? Explain.

3. The ratio of adults to children at a picnic is 4 to 5. The total number of people at the picnic is between 20 and 30. Write an equivalent ratio to find how many adults and children are at the picnic.

4. A recipe for fruit punch calls for 2 cups of pineapple juice for every 3 cups of orange juice. Write an equivalent ratio to find how many cups of pineapple juice should be used with 12 cups of orange juice.

Choose the letter for the best answer.

5. A clothing store stocks 5 blouses for every 3 pairs of pants. Which ratio is proportional for the number of pairs of pants to blouses?

   A 15:9   C 12:20

   B 3:8   D 18:25

6. To make lemonade, you can mix 4 teaspoons of lemonade powder with 16 ounces of water. What is the ratio of powder to water?

   F 4:32   H 24:64

   G 32:8   J 32:128

7. The town library is open 4 days per week. Suppose you use the ratio of days open to days in a week to find the number of days open in 5 weeks. What proportion could you write?

   A $\frac{4}{7} = \frac{20}{25}$ C $\frac{4}{7} = \frac{20}{28}$

   B $\frac{7}{4} = \frac{21}{12}$ D $\frac{4}{7} = \frac{20}{35}$

8. At a factory, the ratio of defective parts to total number of parts is 3:200. Which is an equivalent ratio?

   F 6:1000

   H 30:1000

   G 150:10,000

   J 1,000:10,000

Holt McDougal Mathematics

LESSON 4-4

Problem Solving
Solving Proportions

Write the correct answer.

1. Euros are currency used in several European countries. On one day in October 2005, you could exchange $3 for about 2.5 euros. How many dollars would you have needed to get 8 Euros?

_____

2. A 3-ounce serving of tuna fish provides 24 grams of protein. How many grams of protein are in a 10-ounce serving of tuna fish?

_____

3. Hooke's law states that the distance a spring is stretched is directly proportional to the force applied. If 20 pounds of force stretches a spring 4 inches, how much will the spring stretch if 80 pounds of force is applied?

_____

4. Beeswax used in making candles is produced by honeybees. The honeybees produce 7 pounds of honey for each pound of wax they produce. How many pounds of honey is produced if 145 pounds of beeswax?

_____

Choose the letter for the best answer.

5. For every 5 books her students read, Mrs. Fenway gives them a free homework pass for 4 days. Juan has accumulated homework passes for 12 days so far. What proportion would you write to find how many books Juan has read?

A $\dfrac{4}{12} = \dfrac{x}{5}$

B $\dfrac{4}{5} = \dfrac{x}{12}$

C $\dfrac{4}{5} = \dfrac{12}{x}$

D $\dfrac{5}{12} = \dfrac{4}{x}$

6. In his last 13 times at bat in the township baseball league, Santiago got 8 hits. If he is at bat 65 times for the season, how many hits will he get if his average stays the same?

F $\dfrac{8}{65} = \dfrac{x}{13}$

G $\dfrac{x}{65} = \dfrac{13}{8}$

H $\dfrac{8}{x} = \dfrac{65}{13}$

J $\dfrac{8}{13} = \dfrac{x}{65}$

7. A 12-pack of 8-ounce juice boxes costs $5.40. How much would an 18-pack of juice boxes cost if it is proportionate in price?

A $9.40   C $3.60

B $8.10   D $12.15

8. Jeanette can swim 105 meters in 70 seconds. How far can she probably swim in 30 seconds?

F 20 meters   H 45 meters

G 245 meters   J 55 meters

Holt McDougal Mathematics

Problem Solving

LESSON 4-5

Customary Measurements

Write the correct answer.

1. In 2003, a popcorn sculpture of King Kong was displayed in London. The sculpture was 13 ft tall and 8.75 ft wide. How many inches wide was the sculpture?

_____

2. A pilot whale weighs 1500 lb. A walrus weighs 1.6 tons. Which weighs more? How much more?

_____

3. A zoo has a rhesus monkey that weighed 20 lb. The monkey became sick and lost 18 oz. What was the monkey's new weight?

_____

4. Two containers have capacities of 192 fl oz and 1.25 gal. Which container has a greater capacity? How much greater?

_____

Choose the letter for the best answer.

This table gives lengths and weights for some apes.

Apes		
Name	**Maximum Height**	**Maximum Weight**
Chimpanzee	4 ft	115 lb
Gorilla	67.2 in.	0.2 tons
Orangutan	1.5 yd	3200 oz
Siamang	36 in.	240 oz

7. Which ape has a maximum weight of 200 lb?

   A Chimpanzee

   B Gorilla

   C Orangutan

   D Siamang

5. Which ape has the greatest weight?

   A Chimpanzee

   B Gorilla

   C Orangutan

   D Siamang

6. Which ape has the least height?

   F Chimpanzee

   G Gorilla

   H Orangutan

   J Siamang

8. Which two apes have a 6-inch difference in height?

   F Chimpanzee and gorilla

   G Gorilla and orangutan

   H Siamang and chimpanzee

   J Orangutan and chimpanzee

Holt McDougal Mathematics

LESSON 4-6

Problem Solving
Metric Measurements

Write the correct answer.

1. A porcupine has a mass of 27 kg. A cat has a mass of 6,300 g. Which animal has the greater mass?

2. A faucet drips at the rate of 50 L per day. At this rate, how many days will it take for the faucet to drip a total of 1 kL?

3. The distance from Midwood Library to Midwood Middle School is 0.845 km. The distance from Midwood High School to Midwood Library is 872 m. Which school is closer to the library? How much closer?

4. A mouse has a mass of 18 g. A guinea pig has a mass of 0.85 kg. Is the mass of the two animals together greater or less than 1 kg? Explain your answer.

Choose the letter for the best answer.

The table shows the lengths and masses of some members of the cat family.

Members of the Cat Family		
Name	**Length**	**Mass**
Bobcat	864 mm	18,200 g
Jaguar	1.52 m	55 kg
Canada Lynx	91.4 cm	15,900 g
Mountain Lion	1.35 m	85 kg

7. What is the difference in mass between the cat with the greatest mass and the cat with the least mass?

   A 66.8 kg

   B 69.1 kg

   C 7,400 g

   D 15,815 g

5. Which cat has the greatest length?

   A bobcat

   B jaguar

   C Canada lynx

   D mountain lion

6. Which cat has the least mass?

   F bobcat

   G jaguar

   H Canada lynx

   J mountain lion

8. For which two cats is the difference in length closest to 0.5 m?

   F bobcat and mountain lion

   G bobcat and Canada lynx

   H jaguar and mountain lion

   J jaguar and Canada lynx

Name _____ Date _____ Class _____

Problem Solving

Dimensional Analysis

Use the following: 1 mile = 1.609 km; 1 kg = 2.2046 lb. Round to the nearest tenth.

1. Chinook salmon travel up to 3,000 km to find spawning grounds. How far will a Chinook salmon travel in miles?

   _____

2. Chinook salmon can travel at 23 km/h. How fast can the Chinook salmon travel in miles per hour?

   _____

3. The average rhinoceros weighs 1600 kg. How many pounds does the average rhinoceros weigh?

   _____

4. An adult rhinoceros can have a horn that weighs 3.5 kg. How many pounds do these horns weigh?

   _____

Paraceratherium was the biggest land mammal there has ever been. It lived about 35 million years ago and was 11 m long. The blue whale is the largest mammal that has ever lived. It can be as long as 33 m. 1 foot = 0.3048 meters. Round to the nearest tenth.

5. How long is the blue whale in feet?

   _____

6. How long was the paraceratherium in feet?

   _____

Round to the nearest tenth. Choose the letter for the best answer.

7. The world's fastest bird is the peregrine falcon that flies up to 200 mi an hour. How fast is the peregrine falcon in feet each second?

   A 136.4 ft/s   C 543.2 ft/s

   B 293.3 ft/s   D 9,680 ft/s

8. The longest gloved fight between two Americans lasted for more than seven hours before being declared a draw. How many seconds did the fight last?

   F 127 s   H 420 s

   G 385 s   J 25,200 s

9. The average person showers for eight minutes. How many seconds does it take the average person to shower?

   A 127 s   C 480 s

   B 385 s   D 28,800 s

10. The brain of an average adult female weighs 49 oz. How many pounds does the average female brain weigh?

    F 3.1 lb   H 13.8 lb

    G 5.8 lb   J 784 lb

    Holt McDougal Mathematics

Problem Solving

LESSON 4-8

Similar Figures and Proportions

Use the information in the table to solve problems 1–3.

1. A small reproduction of one of the paintings in the list is similar in size. The reproduction measures 11 inches by 10 inches. Of which painting is this a reproduction?

   _____

Painting	Artist	Original Size (in.)
Mona Lisa	Leonardo da Vinci	30 by 21
The Dance Class	Edgar Degas	33 by 30
The Blue Vase	Paul Cézanne	22 by 18

2. A local artist painted a reproduction of Cézanne's painting. It measures 88 inches by 72 inches. Is the reproduction similar to the original? What is the ratio of corresponding sides?

   _____

3. A poster company made a poster of da Vinci's painting. The poster is 5 feet long and 3.5 feet wide. Is the poster similar to the original *Mona Lisa*? What is the ratio of corresponding sides?

   _____

Choose the letter for the best answer.

4. Triangle *ABC* has sides of 15 cm, 20 cm, and 25 cm. Which triangle could be similar to triangle *ABC*?

   A A triangle with sides of 3 cm, 4 cm, and 5 cm

   B A triangle with sides of 5 cm, 6 cm, and 8 cm

   C A triangle with sides of 30 cm, 40 cm, and 55 cm

   D A triangle with sides of 5 cm, 10 cm, and 30 cm

5. A rectangular picture frame is 14 inches long and 4 inches wide. Which dimensions could a similar picture frame have?

   F Length = 21 in.; width = 8 in.

   G Length = 35 in.; width = 15 in.

   H Length = 49 in.; width = 14 in.

   J Length = 7 in.; width = 3 in.

6. A rectangle is 12 meters long and 21 meters wide. Which dimensions correspond to a nonsimilar rectangle?

   A 4 m; 7 m   C 20 m; 35 m

   B 8 m; 14 m   D 24 m; 35 m

7. A rectangle is 6 feet long and 15 feet wide. Which dimensions correspond to a similar rectangle?

   F 8 ft; 24 ft   H 15 ft; 35 ft

   G 10 ft; 25 ft   J 18 ft; 40 ft

Holt McDougal Mathematics

LESSON	**Problem Solving**
4-9	*Using Similar Figures*

Write the correct answer.

1. An architect is building a model of a tennis court for a new client. On the model, the court is 6 inches wide and 13 inches long. An official tennis court is 36 feet wide. What is the length of a tennis court?

_____

2. Mr. Hemley stands next to the Illinois Centennial Monument at Logan Square in Chicago and casts a shadow that is 18 feet long. The shadow of the monument is 204 feet long. If Mr. Hemley is 6 feet tall, how tall is the monument?

_____

3. The official size of a basketball court in the NBA is 94 feet by 50 feet. The basketball court in the school gym is 47 feet long. How wide must it be to be similar to an NBA court?

_____

4. Two rectangular desks are similar. The larger one is 42 inches long and 18 inches wide. The smaller one is 35 inches long. What is the width of the smaller desk?

_____

Choose the letter for the best answer.

5. An isosceles triangle has two sides that are equal in length. Isosceles triangle *ABC* is similar to isosceles triangle *XYZ*. What proportion would you use to find the length of the third side of triangle *XYZ*?

A $\dfrac{BC}{XZ} = \dfrac{AB}{XY}$ C $\dfrac{AB}{XY} = \dfrac{AC}{XZ}$

B $\dfrac{AC}{XY} = \dfrac{BC}{XZ}$ D $\dfrac{AB}{XY} = \dfrac{BC}{YZ}$

6. The dining room at Monticello, Thomas Jefferson's home in Virginia, is 216 inches by 222 inches. Of the following, which size rug would be similar in shape to the dining room?

   F 72 inches by 74 inches

   G 108 inches by 110 inches

   H 118 inches by 111 inches

   J 84 inches by 96 inches

7. A 9-foot street sign casts a 12-foot shadow. The lamppost next to it casts a 24-foot shadow. How tall is the lamppost?

   A 24 feet

   B 15 feet

   C 18 feet

   D 36 feet

Holt McDougal Mathematics

LESSON 4-10 Problem Solving
Scale Drawings and Scale Models

Write the correct answer.

1. The scale on a road map is 1 cm:500 mi. If the distance on the map between New York City and Memphis is 2.2 centimeters, what is the actual distance between the two cities?

   _____

2. There are several different scales in model railroading. Trains designated as O gauge are built to a scale factor of 1:48. To the nearest hundredth of a foot, how long is a model of a 50-foot boxcar in O gauge?

   _____

3. For a school project, LeeAnn is making a model of the Empire State Building. She is using a scale of 1 cm:8 ft. The Empire State Building is 1,252 feet tall. How tall is her model?

   _____

4. A model of the Eiffel Tower that was purchased in a gift shop is 29.55 inches tall. The actual height of the Eiffel Tower is 985 feet, or 11,820 inches. What scale factor was used to make the model?

   _____

Choose the letter for the best answer.

5. The scale factor for Maria's dollhouse furniture is 1:8. If the sofa in Maria's dollhouse is $7\frac{1}{2}$ inches long, how long is the actual sofa?

   A 54 inches   C 84 inches

   B 60 inches   D $15\frac{1}{2}$ inches

6. The Painted Desert is a section of high plateau extending 150 miles in northern Arizona. On a map, the length of this desert is 5 centimeters. What is the map scale?

   F 1 centimeter:25 miles

   G 5 centimeters:100 miles

   H 1 centimeter:30 miles

   J 1 centimeter:50 miles

7. Josh wants to add a model of a tree to his model railroad layout. How big should the model tree be if the actual tree is 315 inches and the scale factor is 1:90?

   A 395 inches

   B 39.5 inches

   C 35 inches

   D 3.5 inches

8. The scale on a wall map is 1 in:55 mi. What is the distance on the map between two cities that are 99 miles apart?

   F 44 inches

   G 1.8 inches

   H 2.5 inches

   J 0.55 inches

Holt McDougal Mathematics

LESSON 5-1

Problem Solving

The Coordinate Plane

Write the correct answer.

1. Use the coordinate plane at right. In which quadrant(s) would the figure drawn by connecting points *J*, *K*, and *N* be?

   _____

2. Use the coordinate plane at right. In which quadrant(s) would the figure drawn by connecting points *C*, *F*, and *M* be?

   _____

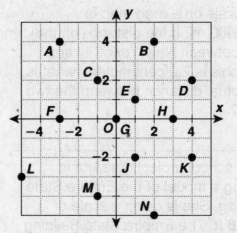

3. Maxine left home and walked 5 blocks north, 5 blocks west, 5 blocks south, and 5 blocks east. Where did she end up?

   _____

4. Mr. Chin drove 2 miles north, then 3 miles east, then 2 miles south. How far is Mr. Chin from where he started?

   _____

Choose the letter for the best answer.

5. Which one of these points lies in Quadrant II of the coordinate plane?

   A (5, 1)   C (−5, 1)

   B (5, −1)   D (−5, −1)

6. In which quadrant of the coordinate plane is the figure formed by joining (−4, −5), (−2, −3) and (−1, −1)?

   F Quadrant I   H Quadrant III

   G Quadrant II   J Quadrant IV

7. Abe and Carlos left the library at the same time. Abe walked 4 blocks north and 5 blocks west. Carlos walked 4 blocks east and 4 blocks north. How far apart were they?

   A 10 blocks   C 8 blocks

   B 9 blocks   D 5 blocks

8. When a point lies on the *x*-axis, which of these must be true?

   F The *x*-coordinate is 0.

   G The *y*-coordinate is 0.

   H The *x*-coordinate is greater than the *y*-coordinate.

   J The *y*-coordinate is greater than the *x*-coordinate.

Holt McDougal Mathematics

LESSON 5-2

Problem Solving

Interpreting Graphs

Write the correct answer.

Eduardo exercises by doing laps around a track. He sprints the straight-aways and walks the curves.

Eduardo's Exercise Routine

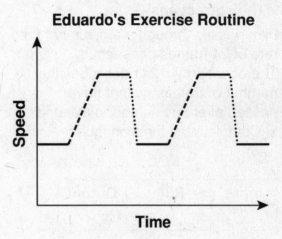

1. What action is represented by the lower horizontal lines in the graph?

   _____

2. What action is represented by the higher horizontal lines in the graph?

   _____

3. What action is represented by the dashed lines in the graph?

   _____

4. What action is represented by the dotted lines in the graph?

   _____

Choose the letter of the best answer.

5. What situation could this graph represent?

   A cost of birdseed by the pound

   B weight of bags of birdseed

   C ages of birds eating birdseed

   D a buy-one-get-one-free sale

   Bird Seed

   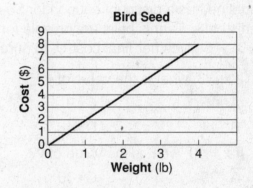

6. What would you expect to pay if you needed $3\frac{1}{2}$ pounds of birdseed?

   F $3.50

   G $5.00

   H $7.00

   J $7.50

7. What is the price for each pound of birdseed?

   A $0.25

   B $0.50

   C $1.00

   D $2.00

Holt McDougal Mathematics

LESSON
5-3

Problem Solving

Functions, Tables, and Graphs

Write the correct answer.

1. Film passes through a projector at the rate of 24 frames per second. The equation $y = 24x$ describes the number of frames, y, that have passed over any number of seconds, x. Complete the function table.

Input	Rule	Output
x		y
2		48
3		72
4		96
5		120
6		144

2. Anne pays $40 a month for cable TV, plus $4 for each movie she watches on pay-per-view channels. Complete the function table, where x is the number of pay-per-view movies she watches each month and y is her monthly cable bill.

Input	Rule	Output
x		y
3		52
5		60
7		68
9		76
11		84

Choose the letter of the best answer.

Madeline has a discount coupon for $5 off her next purchase of tennis balls. Tennis balls are on sale for $3 per can. The equation $y = 3x - 5$ gives her final cost, y, to purchase x cans of tennis balls.

3. If $x = 3$, what is the value of y?

   A 15   C 9
   B 14   D 4

4. If $x = 5$, what is the value of y?

   F 25   H 10
   G 15   J 5

5. If $x = 10$, what is the value of y?

   A 25   C 35
   B 30   D 50

6. If $x = 4$, what is the value of y?

   F 5   H 12
   G 7   J 17

7. If $x = 9$, what is the ordered pair (x, y)?

   A (5, 9)   C (9, 22)
   B (9, 5)   D (9, 10)

8. If $x = 6$, what is the ordered pair (x, y)?

   F (6, 18)   H (12, 31)
   G (6, 30)   J (6, 13)

Holt McDougal Mathematics

LESSON 5-4 Problem Solving
Sequences

Write the correct answer.

1. Marina earns $15 for 1 hour of babysitting, $23 for 2 hours of babysitting, and $31 for 3 hours of babysitting. Write a function to describe the sequence.

2. A website has 175 hits during its first hour of operation. It has 350 hits during its second hour and 525 hits during its third hour. Write a function to describe the sequence.

3. Rodney had 53 baseball cards. Then he started to buy cards each week. After 1 week, Rodney had 73 cards. After 2 weeks, he had 93 cards. After 3 weeks, he had 113 cards. Write a function to describe the sequence. Then use it to predict the number of cards Rodney will have after 5 weeks.

4. Jen is reading a novel that is 463 pages long. After the first day, she had 423 pages left. After 2 days, she had 383 pages left. After 3 days, she had 343 pages left. Write a function to describe the sequence, and use it to predict the number of pages that Jen will have left after 8 days.

Choose the letter of the best answer.

Use the sequence 3, 6, 9, 12, ... for the following exercises.

5. What is the rule for this sequence?

   A Add 3 to n.

   B Subtract 3 from n.

   C Multiply n by 3.

   D Divide n by 3.

6. What is the function that describes this sequence?

   F $y = 3n$

   G $y = \dfrac{n}{3}$

   H $y = n + 3$

   J $y = n - 3$

7. What are the next 3 terms in the sequence?

   A 9, 6, 3

   B 15, 18, 21

   C 15, 19, 24

   D 36, 432, 5,184

8. What is the ninth term in the sequence?

   F 24

   G 27

   H 30

   J 33

Holt McDougal Mathematics

Problem Solving
Graphing Linear Functions

Write the correct answer.

This graph shows the approximate population density (people per square mile) in the United States from 1950 to 2000.

1. Based on this graph, do you think the population of the United States is growing, shrinking, or staying about the same?

   _____

2. How do you know that this is the graph of a linear function?

   _____

   _____

3. On average, by about how many people did the density increase every ten years?

   _____

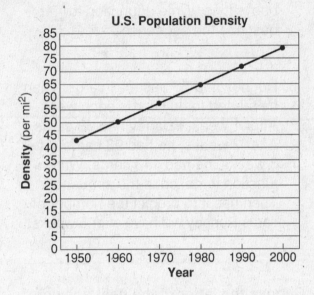

U.S. Population Density

Density (per mi²) / Year

4. Estimate the population density in 2010.

   _____

5. Estimate the population density in 2050.

   _____

Choose the letter of the best answer.

6. Given the linear equation $y = 4x + 1$ and the input $x = 3$, what is the resulting ordered pair?

   A (15, 3)   C (12, 3)

   B (3, 13)   D (12, 11)

7. Given the linear equation $y = \frac{1}{3}x - 4$ and the input $x = 6$, what is the resulting ordered pair?

   F (6, –2)   H (–3, 6)

   G (6, 2)   J $\left(\frac{1}{3}, 6\right)$

8. A technician is adding chemicals to a 210-liter tank. She is adding the liquid at a rate of 2.5 liters per minute. How long will it take to fill the tank half full?

   A 42 min   C 168 min

   B 84 min   D 525 min

9. A basic set of 4 golf lessons costs $95.00. Additional lessons can be purchased at the discounted rate of $15.00 each. What will Veronica pay for a series of 10 lessons?

   F $150   H $185

   G $155   J $245

Holt McDougal Mathematics

Problem Solving

Slope and Rates of Change

Write the correct answer.

1. How much does Jerry earn per hour?

   _____

2. What is the slope of the graph that represents Daniel's rate of pay? How much does Daniel earn per hour?

   _____

3. Jerry and Daniel each worked 10 hours this week. How much more than Daniel did Jerry earn?

   _____

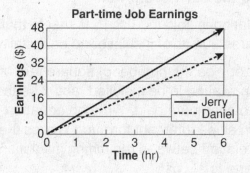

4. For more than 10 hours of work, the rate of pay is 1.5 times that shown in the graph. How much would Jerry earn by working 14 hours?

   _____

Choose the letter of the best answer.

The graph shows the changing height of two rockets over time. Use the graph to solve problems 5 and 6.

5. Which statement is true?

   A Both Rocket A and Rocket B have a constant rate of change in height.

   B Both Rocket A and Rocket B have a variable rate of change in height.

   C Rocket A has a variable rate of change in height, but Rocket B does not.

   D Rocket B has a variable rate of change in height, but Rocket A does not.

6. How fast is the height of rocket B increasing?

   F 5 feet per second

   G 10 feet per second

   H 20 feet per second

   J 40 feet per second

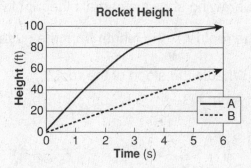

7. Jamaal plotted the point (1, −2). Then he used the slope $-\dfrac{2}{3}$ to find another point on the line. Which point could be the point that Jamaal found?

   A (−1, −1)

   B (4, 0)

   C (2, −3)

   D (4, −4)

Holt McDougal Mathematics

Problem Solving

Slope-Intercept Form

Write the correct answer.

Insulation is sold in 10 × 15 ft sheets that cost $79.50 each. A job
requires 900 ft² of insulation to be installed.

1. Let y be the number of square feet of
   insulation to be installed, and x be the
   total amount paid. Write an equation
   in slope-intercept form to express the
   relation between remaining insulation
   and total cost.

   _____

2. What is the slope of the function?

   _____

3. What is the y-intercept, and what
   does it represent?

   _____

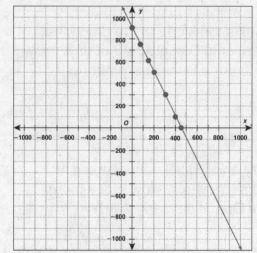

Choose the letter for the best answer.

The drawing shows a partial blueprint for a pitched roof. The height

of the roof is $\frac{1}{3}$ the length from the gutter to point A.

4. What is the slope of the roof?

   A $m = 3$

   B $m = -\frac{1}{3}$

   C $m = \frac{1}{3}$

   D There is no way to tell.

5. If the height of the roof is 14 feet,
   what is the equation of the line?

   F $y = \frac{1}{3}x - 14$

   G $3y = 3x - 14$

   H $y = \frac{14}{3}x + 1$

   J $y = -\frac{1}{3}x + 14$

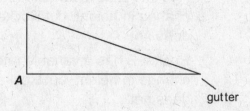

6. If the equation for the roof were
   graphed, which would be a point on
   the graph?

   A (0, 3)   B (0, 0)

   C (3, 13)   D (3, 1)

LESSON 5-8

Problem Solving

Slope-Intercept Form

Write the correct answer.

1. A pipeline delivers 10,422 gallons of natural gas every other month. Tell whether this represents a direct variation. If so, identify the constant of variation and write the equation.

_____

2. A hybrid vehicle gets 31.2 miles per gallon of gas. Complete the data table.

x (gal)	6	9	27
y (mi)			

3. The temperature of a gas increases proportionally with the amount of pressure applied to it. The temperature of propane rises 30 °C for every increase of 4 atm (atmospheres) of pressure. Assume that at 2 atm, the temperature of propane is -30 °C. Make a graph that shows the temperature of the gas at 10 atm of pressure. Is this a direct variation?

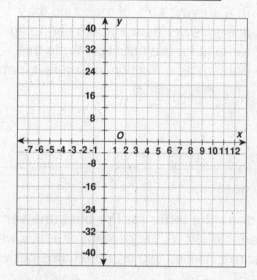

Choose the letter for the best answer.

4. The equation $y = 7x$ shows the rate at which Sara bicycled in m/hi. Which of the following is true?

   A When $y = 4$, $x = 0$.

   B When $x = 7$, $y = 4$.

   C At this rate, Sara would travel 28 miles in 4 hours.

   D At this rate, Sara would travel 4 miles in 28 hours.

5. Which of the following points must the graph of the linear equation $y = 7x$ pass through to represent a direct variation?

   A (0, 1)   C (0, 0)

   B (1, 0)   D (1, 1)

6. Which equation shows the distance y Sara rode if she rode for 5 miles and then started timing her riding at 7 miles per hour, where x is the number of hours she rode?

   A $y = 5x + 7$ C $5y = 7x$

   B $y = 7x + 5$ D $x = 5y + 7$

7. What is the y-intercept of the equation $2x + 3y = 6$?

   A –2   C $\dfrac{2}{3}$

   B $-\dfrac{2}{3}$ D 2

Holt McDougal Mathematics

LESSON 6-1 Problem Solving
Percents

Write the correct answer.

1. In 2003, 68% of the T.V. set owners in the United States had cable television. Write this percent as a fraction in simplest form and as a decimal.

   _____

2. In 2004, 27% of Internet users were in the United States. What percent of Internet users were in countries other than the United States?

   _____

3. In a survey, 46% of men said they spend fewer than 5 hours shopping for gifts for the holidays. Write this percent as a fraction in simplest form and as a decimal.

   _____

4. In a survey, 59% of a group of people aged 18–29 said that they do not have enough time to do what they want. What percent of those surveyed feel that they do have enough time do what they want? Write your answer as a percent and as a decimal.

   _____

Choose the letter for the best answer.
The table shows the percent of adults who participated in selected leisure activities two or more times per week.

5. Express the percent of adults who dined out two or more times per week as a fraction.

   A $\dfrac{1}{100}$ C $\dfrac{1}{10}$

   B $\dfrac{1}{50}$ D $\dfrac{1}{5}$

Adult Participation in Selected Leisure Activities in 2003

Activity	Percent
Crossword puzzles	7%
Dining out	10%
Reading books	21%
Surfing the net	18%
Video games	5%

6. Express the percent of adults who did crossword puzzles two or more times per week as a decimal.

   F 0.07   H 0.5

   G 0.05   J 0.7

7. What fraction of adults played video games fewer than two times per week?

   A $\dfrac{1}{20}$ C $\dfrac{19}{50}$

   B $\dfrac{1}{50}$ D $\dfrac{19}{20}$

8. Which decimal represents the percent of adults who surfed the net fewer than two times per week?

   F 0.018   H 0.18

   G 0.05   J 0.82

Holt McDougal Mathematics

LESSON 6-2 Problem Solving
Fractions, Decimals, and Percents

Write the correct answer.

1. About 543 out of every 1,000 people in the United States owned a cell phone in 2003. In Japan, the rate was 68 for every 100 people. How much greater was the percent of cell phone ownership in Japan than in the U.S.?

2. In 2002, the adult population of the United States was about 206 million. About 113 million people participated in an exercise program. To the nearest percent, what percent of the adult population participated in an exercise program?

3. When asked about their favorite Thanksgiving leftover, $\frac{1}{20}$ of the people said vegetables and $\frac{7}{100}$ said mashed potatoes. Which food was more popular and by what percent?

4. In a survey, 80 people were asked whether they thought the speed limit for interstate highways should be raised. Twenty-five people said the speed limit should be raised. What percent of people did not think that the speed limit should be raised?

Choose the letter for the best answer.

The table shows the number of students in four schools who own computers.

5. What percent of students at Percy owns computers?

  A 125%   C 250%

  B 12.5%   D 25%

6. In which school does about 73% of the students own computers?

  F Hunter   H Percy

  G Madison   J King

7. What percent of students at Madison do not own computers? Round to the nearest tenth of a percent.

  A 3.3%   C 33.3%

  B 9.9%   D 66.7%

Students Who Own Computers

School	Number of Students
Madison	90 out of 270
Hunter	56 out of 100
King	110 out of 150
Percy	125 out of 500

8. Which school has the greatest percent of students who own computers?

  F Hunter   H Percy

  G Madison   J King

         Holt McDougal Mathematics

LESSON
6-3

Problem Solving

Estimating with Percents

Write the correct answer.

Use the graph to solve Exercises 1–3.

1. If a ski resort in the Rocky Mountain region had 125 visitors, about how many would be snowboarders?

   _____

2. Recently at one ski resort, 120 out of 400 guests were snowboarders. In which region is this resort?

   _____

Snowboarding Ski-Resort Visitors

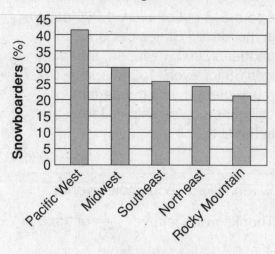

Ski-Resort Region

3. Last year, a ski resort in the Northeast region had an average of 556 visitors per weekend. About how many of them were snowboarders?

   _____

4. A large department store has an average of 3,456 shoppers per day. About 26% of the shoppers buys something in the store. About how many shoppers each day spend money in the store?

   _____

Choose the letter for the best answer.

5. LaToya bought a new car for $29,000. She is entitled to an 11% rebate. About how much will the car cost after the rebate?

   A $3,000   C $22,000

   B $10,000   D $26,000

6. The cost of a video game is $29.95. Sales tax is 6%. About how much will the video game cost, including tax?

   F about $29   H about $32

   G about $30   J about $35

7. In 2004, the Brooklyn Public Library spent about $7.6 million on acquisitions. The Detroit Public Library spent about 26% of that amount. About how much money did the Detroit Public Library spend?

   A $2 million   C $8 million

   B $3 million   D $26 million

8. In 2002, the average starting salary of a high school teacher in Switzerland was $48,704. The average starting salary of a high school teacher in the United States was about 61% of that amount. About how much was the average starting salary in the U.S?

   F $6,000   H $30,000

   G $24,000   J $60,000

LESSON
6-4

Problem Solving
Percent of a Number

Write the correct answer.

The world population is estimated to exceed 9 billion by the year 2050. Use the circle graph to solve Exercises 1–3.

1. What is the estimated population of Africa in the year 2050?

   _____

2. Which continent is estimated to have more than 5.31 billion people by the year 2050?

   _____

3. In the year 2002, the world population was estimated at 6 billion people. Based on research from the World Bank, about 20% lived on less than $1 per day. How many people lived on less than $1 per day?

   _____

Estimated 2050 World Population

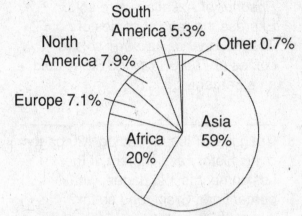

4. What is the combined estimated population for North and South America by the year 2050?

   _____

Choose the letter for the best answer.

5. The student population at King Middle School is 52% female. The total student population is 1,225 students. How many boys go to King Middle School?

   A 538 boys   C 637 boys
   B 588 boys   D 1,173 boys

6. There are 245 students in the seventh grade. If 40% of them ride the bus to school, how many seventh graders do not ride the bus to school?

   F 98 students   H 185 students
   G 147 students   J 205 students

7. A half-cup of pancake mix has 5% of the total daily allowance of cholesterol. The total daily allowance of cholesterol is 300 mg. How much cholesterol does a half-cup of pancake mix have?

   A 100 mg   C 20 mg
   B 60 mg   D 15 mg

8. Carey needs $45 to buy her mother a birthday present. She has saved 22% of the amount so far. How much more does she need?

   F $35.10   H $23.00
   G $44.01   J $9.90

LESSON 6-5

Problem Solving

Solving Percent Problems

Write the correct answer.

1. At one time during 2001, for every 20 copies of *Harry Potter and the Sorcerer's Stone* that were sold, 13.2 copies of *Harry Potter and the Prisoner of Azkaban* were sold. Express the ratio of copies of *The Prisoner of Azkaban* sold to copies of *The Sorcerer's Stone* sold as a percent.

_____

2. A souvenir mug sells for $8.00 at a hotel gift store. Kendra gives the clerk $9.00 and receives $0.56 in change. What is the sales tax rate?

_____

3. Craig just finished reading 120 pages of his history assignment. If the assignment is 125 pages, what percent has Craig read so far?

_____

4. Hal's Sporting Goods had a 1-day sale. The original price of a mountain bike was $325. On sale, it was $276.25. What is the percent reduction for this sale?

_____

Choose the correct letter for the best answer.

5. China's area is about 3.7 million square miles. It is on the continent of Asia, which has an area of about 17.2 million square miles. About what percent of the Asian continent does China cover?

  A about 10%   C about 17%

  B about 15%   D about 22%

6. After six weeks, the tomato plant that was given extra plant food and water was 26 centimeters tall. The tomato plant that was not given any extra plant food was only 74.5% as tall. How tall was the tomato plant that was not given extra plant food?

  F 1.94 cm   H 34.89 cm

  G 19.37 cm   J 48.5 cm

7. In a survey, 46 people, which was 20% of those surveyed, chose red as their favorite color. How many people were surveyed?

  A 66 people   C 460 people

  B 230 people   D 920 people

8. Of the 77 billion food and drink cans, bottles, and jars Americans throw away each year, about 65% of them are cans. How many food and drink cans, to the nearest billion, do Americans throw away each year?

  F 12 billion   H 50 billion

  G 17 billion   J 65 billion

Holt McDougal Mathematics

LESSON 6-6

Problem Solving
Percent of Change

Write the correct answer.

1. In 2002, U.S. consumers bought about 8.1 million new cars. In 2003, that number decreased by about 6%. To the nearest hundred thousand, or tenth of a million, how many new cars did U.S. consumers buy in 2003?

2. In Union County, Florida, the 1990 census listed the population at 10,252. The 2000 census listed the population as 13,442. What percent increase is this to the nearest tenth of a percent?

3. World production of motor vehicles increased from about 60 million in 2002 to 62 million in 2003. What was the percent increase to the nearest percent?

4. Arthur's dog, Shep, used to weigh 158 pounds. The vet put him on a diet and he lost 13% of his weight. To the nearest pound, how much does Shep weigh now?

5. The number of volunteers rose from 47 on Monday to 64 on Tuesday. What is the percent increase to the nearest tenth of a percent?

6. Coretta's bowling average decreased from 158 to 133. What is the percent decrease to the nearest tenth of a percent?

Choose the correct letter for the best answer.

7. Shandra scored 75 on her first math test. She scored 20% higher on her next math test. What did she score on the second test?

   A 80   C 90

   B 85   D 95

8. Jim's Gym had income of $20,350 last month. The total increased by $2,000 this month. What was the percent increase to the nearest percent?

   F 11%   H 7%

   G 10%   J 6%

9. Last year, the average number of absences in school was 8 students per day. This year, the absentee rate is down to 6 students per day. What is the percent decrease in student absences this year?

   A 75%   C 25%

   B 33%   D 66%

10. During the 2002–2003 ski season $171 million worth of snowboarding equipment was sold. Sales increased by about 15% during the 2003–2004 season. About how much were sales of snowboarding equipment in the 2003–2004 season?

   F $145 million   H $186 million

   G $156 million   J $197 million

Holt McDougal Mathematics

LESSON 6-7

Problem Solving

Simple Interest

Write the correct answer.

Use the graph to solve Exercises 1–3.

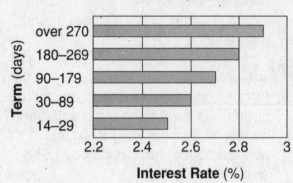

AEA Bank Simple Interest CDs

Term (days): over 270, 180–269, 90–179, 30–89, 14–29

Interest Rate (%)

1. How much more interest would be earned on a $100,000 CD for 9 months than for 6 months?

_____

2. A customer earned $3,262.50 interest on a 9-month CD. How much was the opening deposit?

_____

3. Mrs. Wallace bought a $125,000 CD with a term of 3 years. How much will she earn in 3 years?

_____

4. Until June 2002, the simple interest rate on Stafford loans to college students was 5.39% while the student was still in college. How much interest would a student pay on a $1,500 loan for 2 years?

_____

5. Diego deposits $4,200 into a savings account that pays 5% simple interest. He decides not to touch the money until it doubles. How long will Diego have to keep the money in this account?

_____

Choose the letter of the best answer.

6. Scott took out a 4-year car loan for $5,500. He paid back a total of $7,370. What interest rate did he pay for this loan?

   A 9.5%   C 8.5%

   B 9%   D 7.5%

7. How much interest would you earn if you were to deposit $575 for 3 months at 2.88% simple interest?

   F $4.14   H $41.40

   G $4.83   J $48.30

8. How long would you need to keep $775 in an account that pays 3% simple interest to earn $93 interest?

   A 4 years   C 4 months

   B 2 years   D 2 months

9. If you borrow $12,000 for 30 months at 6.5% simple interest, what is the total amount you will have to repay?

   F $12,065   H $13,950

   G $12,780   J $21,500

Holt McDougal Mathematics

Problem Solving
Frequency Tables, Stem-and-Leaf Plots, and Line Plots

LESSON 7-1

Write the correct answer.

The table shows the time in minutes that Naima talked on the phone during the last 3 weeks.

Phone Time (min)

	Mon	Tues	Wed	Thurs	Fri	Sat	Sun
Week 1	12	15	25	45	52	30	31
Week 2	22	25	46	51	10	19	33
Week 3	44	21	30	20	10	24	52

1. Naima made a cumulative frequency table of the data using equal intervals. What number would she write in the frequency column for the interval 11–20 minutes?

2. Naima made a line plot of the data. Which numbers had more than one X above them?

3. If Naima makes a stem-and-leaf plot, which stem has the most leaves? What are they?

4. In the stem-and-leaf plot, which stems have the same number of leaves?

The list shows Hank Aaron's season home run totals. Make a cumulative frequency table, stem-and-leaf plot, and a line plot for the data. Then use the data to solve problems 5–8.

13, 27, 26, 44, 30, 39, 40, 34, 45, 44, 24, 32
44, 39, 29, 44, 38, 47, 34, 40, 20, 12, 10

5. In a cumulative frequency table of the data, what number belongs in the frequency column for interval 40-44?
   - A 5
   - B 6
   - C 8
   - D 14

6. In a cumulative frequency table of the data, what number belongs in the frequency column for interval 25-29?
   - F 3
   - G 5
   - H 6
   - J 8

7. In a stem-and-leaf plot of the data, how many stems do you need?
   - A 1
   - B 2
   - C 3
   - D 4

8. In a line plot of the data, which number would have 4 x's above it?
   - F 34
   - G 40
   - H 44
   - J 45

LESSON 7-2

Problem Solving

Mean, Median, Mode, and Range

Write the correct answer.

The table to the right shows the leading shot blockers in the WNBA during the 2003 season.

Player	Shots Blocked
Margo Dydek	100
Lauren Jackson	64
Lisa Leslie	63
Ruth Riley	58
Michelle Snow	62

1. What is the range of this set of data?

_____

2. What are the mean, median, and mode of this set of data?

3. What is the outlier in this set of data?

_____

4. How does the outlier affect the mean and the median?

_____

_____

5. Which measure of central tendency best describes the set of data with the outlier? Explain.

_____

_____

Choose the letter for the best answer.

In a 100-meter dash, the first 5 racers finished with the following times: 11.6 seconds, 13.4 seconds, 10.8 seconds, 11.8 seconds, and 13.4 seconds.

6. Which measure of central tendency for this set of data is 12.2 seconds?

   A   mean

   B   median

   C   mode

   D   none of the above

7. Which measure of central tendency for this set of data is 11.8 seconds?

   F   mean

   G   median

   H   mode

   J   none of the above

8. What is the mode for this set of data?

   A   10.8 seconds

   B   11.8 seconds

   C   13.4 seconds

   D   none of the above

9. The sixth racer finished with a time of 16.4 seconds. How will that affect the mean for this set of data?

   F   decrease it by 0.7 second

   G   increase it by 0.7 second

   H   increase it by 3.28 seconds

   J   does not affect the mean

Holt McDougal Mathematics

LESSON 7-3

Problem Solving
Bar Graphs and Histograms

Write the correct answer.

The double-bar graph shows the win-loss records for the Carolina
Panthers football team in the years 1998–2004.

1. During how many seasons did the
   Panthers lose more games than they
   won?

   _____

2. In which year did the Panthers win
   more games than they lost?

   _____

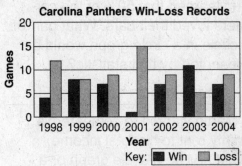

Carolina Panthers Win-Loss Records

Key: ■ Win   □ Loss

3. Between which 2 years did the
   Panthers have the greatest
   improvement in their win-loss record?

   _____

4. In which year do you find the greatest
   range in the win-loss record?

   _____

Choose the letter for the best answer.

The histogram shows the ages of all members in a fan club.

5. How many fan club members could
   be teenagers?

   A 5   C 17

   B 8   D 21

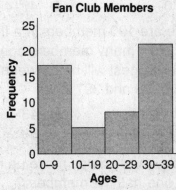

Fan Club Members

6. How many fan club members are
   between the ages of 30 and 39?

   F 5   H 17

   G 8   J 22

7. In which situation would you use a
   histogram to display data?

   A to show how you spend money

   B to show the change in
      temperature throughout the day

   C to show the golf scores from the
      whole team

   D to show the life expectancy of
      different animals

8. In which situation would you use a bar
   graph to display data?

   F to compare the speed of different
      computers

   G to show how a cat spends its time

   H to show how a child's height
      changes as he or she grows

   J to show the distribution of math
      grades in your class

Holt McDougal Mathematics

LESSON
7-4

Problem Solving
Reading and Interpreting Circle Graphs

Write the correct answer.

1. A market research group conducted a survey of 100 sports car owners. The group learned that 50% of the car owners loved their cars. What part of the circle in a circle graph would be represented by that statistic?

_____

□2. Juanita has 100 CDs. In her collection, 37 of the CDs are rock music, 25 are jazz, and 38 are country music. What part of the circle in a circle graph would represent the jazz CDs?

_____

3. Mr. Martin wanted to compare his monthly rent to his total income. Should he use a circle graph or a bar graph?

_____

4. Mr. Martin's rent has increased every year for the last 6 years. Should he use a circle graph or bar graph to show the yearly increase?

_____

Choose the letter for the best answer. Use the circle graph.

5. To which age group do most of the fitness club members belong?

   A 18–20   C 30–39

   B 70+   D 40–49

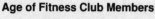
Age of Fitness Club Members

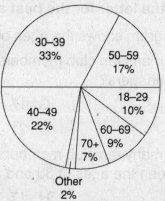

6. There are 100 members in a fitness club. How many members does the graph suggest will be between the ages of 18 and 39?

   F 10   H 43

   G 33   J 22

7. Which 2 age groups make up more than one-half the members?

   A 18–29 and 30–39

   B 30–39 and 40–49

   C 40–49 and 50–59

   D 18–29 and 70+

8. Which 2 age groups make up 3 times as many members as those who are between 60 and 69?

   F 40–49 and 50–59

   G 50–59 and 70+

   H 30–39 and 18–29

   J 18–29 and 50–59

Holt McDougal Mathematics

Problem Solving

LESSON
7-5

Box-and-Whisker Plots

Write the correct answer.

A fitness center offers two different yoga classes. The attendance for each class for 12 sessions is represented in the box-and-whisker plot.

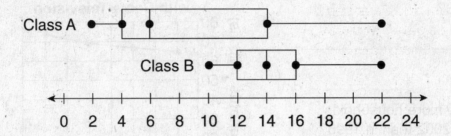

1. Which class has a greater median attendance? How much greater is it?

   _____

2. Which class appears to have a more predictable attendance?

   _____

3. Which class has an attendance of less than 14 people 75% of the time?

   _____

4. What percent of the time does Class B have an attendance greater than 16?

   _____

Choose the letter for the best answer.

The box-and-whisker plot shows the percent of people in eight Central American countries who used the Internet in 2005.

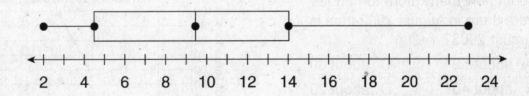

5. What is the range in the percents of people who used the Internet in the eight countries?

   A 23%   C 14%

   B 21%   D 9.5%

6. In how many of these eight countries did at least 9.5% of the people use the Internet?

   F less than 2   H at least 4

   G less than 4   J cannot be determined

7. What is the mode of the data?

   A 2%   C 9.5%

   B 4.5   D cannot be determined

8. What is the interquartile range of the data?

   F 23%   H 14%

   G 21%   J 9.5%

Holt McDougal Mathematics

LESSON 7-6

Problem Solving
Line Graphs

Write the correct answer.
The line graph shows the number of households with cable television from 1996 to 2002.

1. About how many households had cable TV in 1998?

   _____

2. About how many more households had cable TV in 2002 than in 1996?

   _____

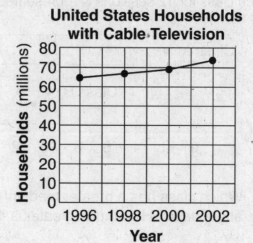

United States Households with Cable Television

3. During which two-year period did the number of households with cable TV grow the most?

   _____

4. Use the graph to estimate the number of households with cable TV in 2001.

   _____

Choose the letter for the best answer.
The double-line graph shows the number of tornadoes in the United States during part of 2002 and 2003.

5. About how many more tornadoes were there in August 2002 than in August 2003?

   A about 50   C about 30

   B about 40   D about 20

6. In which time period did the number of tornadoes increase both years?

   F Sept. to Oct.   H Nov. to Dec.

   G Oct. to Nov.   J none

7. Which time period showed the greatest decrease in the number of tornadoes?

   A Aug. to Sept. 2002

   B Aug. to Sept. 2003

   C Oct. to Nov. 2002

   D Nov. to Dec. 2003

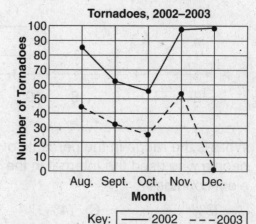

Tornadoes, 2002–2003

Key: ——— 2002   - - - 2003

8. During which month was there the greatest difference between the number of tornadoes in 2002 and in 2003?

   F Aug.   H Nov.

   G Sept.   J Dec.

Holt McDougal Mathematics

LESSON 7-7

Problem Solving
Choosing an Appropriate Display

Write the correct answer.

1. You take a survey of your class to find the number of years each student has lived in your town. You want to show how the data is distributed. What kind of graph would you use to display your data? Explain your choice.

   _____

   _____

   _____

☐2. Wendy budgets $120 for the week. $30 is for transportation, $50 is for food, $25 is for entertainment, and $15 is for other expenses. What kind of graph would best represent the data? Justify your response.

   _____

   _____

   _____

3. The New York Mets' worst season was their first season, in 1962. In that year they won 40 games. Their best season was in 1986, when they won 108 games. You want to show the number of games won each year in a way that makes it easy to see the distribution of the data. Why might you use a stem-and-leaf plot rather than a line plot?

   _____

   _____

   _____

4. During one school year, Matt reads 16 books, Tama reads 22 books, Rhonda reads 14 books, and Francisco reads 20 books. Would a line graph be an appropriate way to display this data? Explain your answer.

   _____

   _____

   _____

Choose the letter for the best answer.

5. Which type of graph would be most appropriate to show the distribution of daily high temperatures for a month?

   A circle graph

   B Venn diagram

   C stem-and-leaf plot

   D line graph

6. Which type of graph would be most appropriate to compare the price of the same TV at five discount stores?

   F stem-and-leaf plot

   G bar graph

   H circle graph

   J line plot

LESSON
7-8
Problem Solving
Populations and Samples

Write the correct answer.

1. Max wants to find out the exercise habits of local children. He plans to survey every third child he sees coming out of a sporting goods store. Max says his sample is not biased. Do you agree? Explain your answer.

_____

_____

_____

2. Ms. Constantine is choosing among three field trips for her two classes. She wants to determine which trip her students prefer. Should she survey the entire population or use a sample? Explain.

_____

_____

_____

3. A researcher catches 60 fish from different locations in a lake. He then tags the fish and puts them back in the lake. Two weeks later, the researcher catches 40 fish from the same locations. 8 of these 40 fish are tagged. Predict the number of fish in the lake.

_____

4. A high school has 1,800 students. A random sample of 80 shows that 24 have cell phones. Predict the number of students in the high school who have cell phones.

_____

Choose the letter for the best answer.

5. The school board wants to study computer literacy among teachers. Which would represent a random sample of teachers?

   A all high school math teachers

   B teachers from the middle school whose name begins with N

   C all male teachers

   D every eighth teacher on an alphabetical list

6. In a random sample, 3 of 400 computer chips are found to be defective. Based on the sample, about how many chips out of 100,000 would you expect to be defective?

   F 750

   G 3,000

   H 4,000

   J cannot be determined

Problem Solving
Scatter Plots

Write the correct answer.

This scatter plot compares the mean annual income of Americans with the number of years spent in school.

1. Which level of education has a mean annual income between $40,000 and $50,000?

   _____

2. Estimate the range of income data on this scatter plot.

   _____

3. Which level of education has the lowest income?

   _____

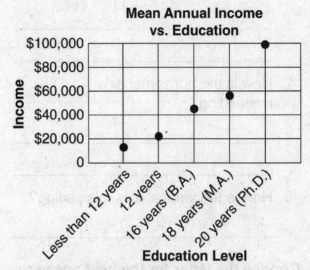

4. Does the scatter plot show a positive correlation, negative correlation, or no correlation between education and income?

   _____

Choose the letter for the best answer.

5. What kind of correlation would you expect to find between a city's annual snowfall amount and the size of its population?

   A positive correlation

   B negative correlation

   C no correlation

   D impossible to say

6. What kind of correlation would you expect to find between a movie's length and the number of times it can be shown in a day?

   F positive correlation

   G negative correlation

   H no correlation

   J impossible to say

7. What kind of correlation would you expect to find between an animal's mass and the number of calories it consumes in a day?

   A positive correlation

   B negative correlation

   C no correlation

   D impossible to say

8. What kind of correlation would you expect to find between a person's height and his or her income?

   F positive correlation

   G negative correlations

   H no correlation

   J impossible to say

LESSON 7-10

Problem Solving

Misleading Graphs

Write the correct answer. Use the line graph for Exercises 1–4.

1. What would be a less misleading title for this graph?

   _____

   _____

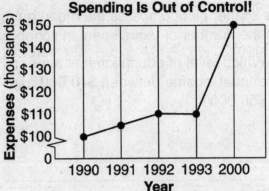

Spending Is Out of Control!

2. How is the horizontal axis misleading?

   _____

   _____

3. How is the vertical axis misleading?

   _____

4. How much did spending really increase between 1993 and 2000?

   _____

Choose the letter for the best answer.

The bar graph is an advertisement used by a tour company to convince New Yorkers to vacation in Hawaii.

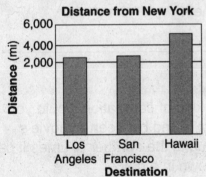

Distance from New York

5. How far is New York from Los Angeles?

   A 2,500 miles   C 5,000 miles

   B 4,000 miles   D 5,200 miles

6. How far is New York from Hawaii?

   F 2,500 miles   H 5,000 miles

   G 2,600 miles   J 6,000 miles

7. What is the point of the ad?

   A New York is closer to Hawaii than to Los Angeles.

   B Hawaii is the same distance from New York as Los Angeles.

   C Hawaii is only slightly farther from New York than is Los Angeles.

   D San Francisco and Los Angeles are the same distance from New York.

8. Why is the graph misleading?

   F The distances are incorrect.

   G The bars are mislabeled.

   H The bars are too tall.

   J The intervals on the vertical axis are not equal.

    Holt McDougal Mathematics

Problem Solving
Building Blocks of Geometry

Write the correct answer.

The drawing shows a section of the Golden Gate Bridge in San Francisco.

1. Identify two lines that are suggested by the bridge.

   _____

2. Identify a ray and a line segment that are suggested by the bridge.

   _____

3. Identify two lines in the figure that are in the same plane.

   _____

4. Identify a plane in the figure.

   _____

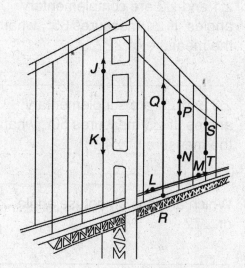

Choose the letter for the best answer.

The drawing is an artist's sketch for an abstract painting.

5. Which line segment is congruent to $\overline{BC}$?

   A $\overline{AB}$ C $\overline{AC}$

   B $\overline{KJ}$ D $\overline{HM}$

6. Which line segment is congruent to $\overline{GM}$?

   F $\overline{AC}$ H $\overline{DE}$

   G $\overline{DF}$ J $\overline{AB}$

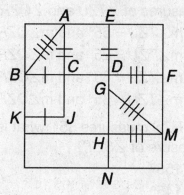

7. Which line segment is congruent to $\overline{ED}$?

   A $\overline{AC}$ C $\overline{DF}$

   B $\overline{CD}$ D $\overline{GH}$

8. Which line segment is congruent to $\overline{DF}$?

   F $\overline{ED}$ H $\overline{CJ}$

   G $\overline{HM}$ J $\overline{FM}$

Holt McDougal Mathematics

Problem Solving
Classifying Angles

Write the correct answer.

The drawing shows a scene on a calendar.

1. ∠1 and ∠2 are complementary angles. If ∠1 measures 35°, what is the measure of ∠2?

   _____

2. ∠3 and ∠4 are supplementary angles. If ∠3 measures 50°, what is the measure of ∠4?

   _____

3. Which angle is an obtuse angle: ∠6 or ∠7?

   _____

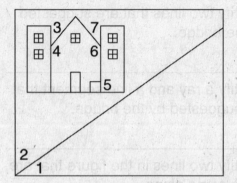

4. Which angle labeled on the drawing is a right angle?

   _____

Choose the letter for the correct answer.

Use the diagram to complete Exercises 5 and 6.

5. Which of the following could be the measures of ∠TZU and ∠QZR?
   A m∠TZU = 55° and m∠QZR = 55°
   B m∠TZU = 25° and m∠QZR = 90°
   C m∠TZU = 80° and m∠QZR = 100°
   D m∠TZU = 35° and m∠QZR = 80°

6. If ∠RZS measures 35°, what is the measure of ∠SZT?
   F 155°
   G 145°
   H 55°
   J 45°

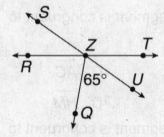

7. ∠A and ∠B are complementary angles. The measure of ∠B is 4 times the measure of ∠A. What are the measures of the angles?
   A m∠A = 16° and m∠B = 64°
   B m∠A = 18° and m∠B = 72°
   C m∠A = 36° and m∠B = 144°
   D m∠A = 45° and m∠B = 135°

8. The hands of a clock form an acute angle at 1:00. What type of angle do they form at 4:00?
   F acute
   G right
   H obtuse
   J straight

Holt McDougal Mathematics

Problem Solving

LESSON 8-3

Line and Angle Relationships

Write the correct answer.

In the drawing of the chair, the seat is parallel to the floor.

1. What is the measure of ∠1?

   _____

2. What is the measure of ∠2?

   _____

3. What is the measure of ∠3?

   _____

4. What is the measure of ∠4?

   _____

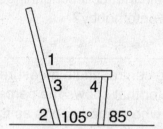

Choose the letter for the best answer.

The map shows the area around Falcon Park. Birch Street and Orchard Street are parallel to each other.

5. If 4 measures 112°, what is the measure of 6?

   A 112°   C 68°

   B 22°   D 108°

6. Which two angles are vertical angles?

   F ∠2 and ∠3   H ∠2 and ∠4

   G ∠2 and ∠6   J ∠2 and ∠5

7. If 10 measures 87°, what is the measure of 9?

   A 77°   C 87°

   B 93°   D 103°

8. Which is a transversal to Birch and Orchard streets?

   F Maple Street H Oak Street

   G Elm Street   J Falcon Park

9. If ∠4 measures 112°, what is the measure of ∠1?

   A 22°   C 108°

   B 68°   D 112°

Holt McDougal Mathematics

LESSON 8-4

Problem Solving
Properties of Circles

Write the correct answer.

The circle graph shows the results of a survey in which people were asked to name their hobbies.

1. If 1,000 people were surveyed, how many said that collecting things is their favorite hobby?

_____

2. Find the central angle measure of the sector that shows the percent of people who named sports as their favorite hobby.

_____

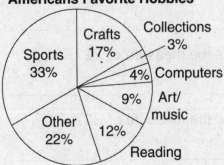

Americans Favorite Hobbies

3. Find the central angle measure of the sector that shows the percent of people who named reading as their favorite hobby.

_____

4. Find the central angle measure of the sector that shows the percent of people who like to do crafts as their favorite hobby.

_____

Choose the letter for the best answer.

The circle graph shows the age breakdown of people who most enjoy snowboarding.

5. What is the central angle measure that shows the percent of 35–54-year-olds?

  A 5.1°   C 23.4°

  B 6.5°   D 40.7°

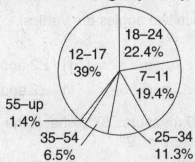

Snowboarding Popularity

6. With which age group is snowboarding least popular?

  F 7–11 years   H 25–34 years

  G 12–17 years   J 55–up

7. With which age group is snowboarding most popular?

  A 7–11 years   C 18–24 years

  B 12–17 years   D 25–34 years

8. What is the central angle measure that shows the percent of 12–17-year-olds?

  F 39°   H 108°

  G 140.4°   J 180°

LESSON 8-5

Problem Solving
Classifying Polygons

Write the correct answer.

The drawing shows a crown designed by a child in an arts and crafts class. The crown is composed of 4 different figures.

1. Name the polygon in figure 1.

   _____

2. Name the polygon in figure 4.

   _____

3. Name the polygon in figure 3.

   _____

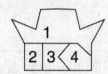

4. Is the crown a regular polygon? Explain.

   _____

   _____

5. Name the polygon formed by figures 2, 3, and 4.

   _____

Choose the letter for the best answer.

The box shows some basic shapes from a word processing tool bar.

6. Which figure is *not* a quadrilateral?

   A Figure 2   C Figure 4
   B Figure 3   D Figure 5

7. Which figure is *not* a polygon?

   F Figure 3   H Figure 11
   G Figure 9   J Figure 12

8. Which figure is a pentagon?

   A Figure 4   C Figure 10
   B Figure 5   D Figure 12

9. Which figure is a regular polygon?

   F Figure 1   H Figure 7
   G Figure 2   J Figure 8

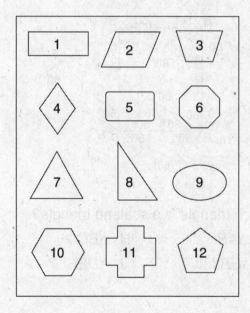

10. Which figure is an octagon?

    A Figure 6   C Figure 11
    B Figure 10   D Figure 12

Holt McDougal Mathematics

Problem Solving

LESSON
8-6

Classifying Triangles

Write the correct answer.

Brian made the following drawing of his kite.

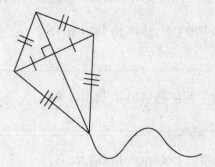

1. How many triangles are in the figure?

   _____

2. How many acute triangles are in the figure?

   _____

3. How many right triangles are in the figure?

   _____

4. How many scalene triangles are in the figure?

   _____

5. How many isosceles triangles are in the figure?

   _____

Choose the letter for the best answer.

The figure shows an architect's design for a large window.

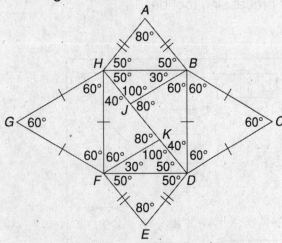

9. Which triangle is a scalene triangle?

   F △ABH   H △BCD

   G △HBJ   J △DEF

6. Which triangle is an equilateral triangle?

   A △ABH   C △FGH

   B △BDH   D △DHF

7. Which triangle is a right triangle?

   F △FHK   H △DKF

   G △DEF   J △DBH

8. Which triangle is an isosceles triangle?

   A △DBJ   C △HBJ

   B △DEF   D △DHF

10. Which triangle is an obtuse triangle?

    A △DKF   C △JBD

    B △HKF   D △ABH

LESSON 8-7

Problem Solving

Classifying Quadrilaterals

Write the correct answer.

1. A garden has 2 pairs of congruent sides. The congruent sides are not adjacent, and the angles are not all congruent. What is the shape of the garden?

2. A poster advertising an art show has 1 pair of parallel sides. All the angles are different, and none of the sides are congruent. What is the shape of this poster?

3. In a math report, Ming said that since a rhombus has 4 equal sides and a square has 4 equal sides, all rhombuses are squares. Is she correct? Explain.

4. A student was asked to give an example of a polygon that is not a quadrilateral and an example of a quadrilateral that is not a polygon. Is this possible? Why or why not?

Choose the letter for the best answer.

5. Which type of quadrilateral do you see most in the painting?

   A rhombus   C rectangle

   B trapezoid   D square

This is a drawing of Piet Mondrian's painting *Composition 8*.

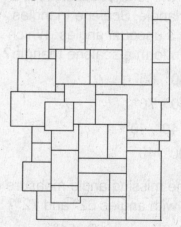

6. Which type of quadrilateral does not appear to be in the painting?

   F rectangle

   G parallelogram

   H square

   J trapezoid

7. Which statement is true about the painting?

   A There are no parallelograms.

   B There are only rectangles.

   C There are only quadrilaterals.

   D None of the above

8. Which statement is true about the painting?

   F There are no triangles.

   G There are only squares.

   H There are no squares.

   J None of the above

Holt McDougal Mathematics

LESSON
8-8

Problem Solving

Angles in Polygons

Write the correct answer.

These are some common street signs.

1. The interior angles of which sign have a sum of 360°?

   _____

2. What is the sum of the interior angles of a stop sign?

   _____

3. The interior angles of which sign have a sum of 540°?

   _____

4. If a yield sign is a regular polygon, what is the measure of each angle?

   _____

Choose the letter for the best answer.

5. A triangle with 3 unequal sides is a scalene triangle. Scalene triangles also have 3 unequal angles. Which angles can form a scalene triangle?

   A 50°, 60°, 65°

   B 50°, 60°, 70°

   C 110°, 40°, 40°

   D 20°, 20°, 40°

6. A design on a belt shows a row of irregular pentagons. Inside each figure, two of the angles each measure 60°. Another angle measures 270°. If the remaining angles are equal, what are their measures?

   F 60° each   H 75° each

   G 120° each   J 150° each

7. What is the missing angle measure of a triangle with angles 62° and 72°?

   A 52°   C 54°

   B 34°   D 46°

8. On a door is a sign that says "Welcome To Our Home." The sign is in the shape of a regular octagon. What is the measure of one of the interior angles of the sign?

   F 135°   H 80°

   G 65°   J 150°

Holt McDougal Mathematics

LESSON 8-9

Problem Solving

Congruent Figures

Write the correct answer.

The table shows the dimensions of regulation NBA and NCAA basketball courts, which are rectangular in shape.

Basketball Court and Lane Sizes

	NBA	NCAA
Court	94 ft by 50 ft	94 ft by 50 ft
Lane	16 ft by 19 ft	12 ft by 19 ft

1. Is an NBA court congruent to an NCAA court? Why or why not?

_____

_____

2. If the lane on an NBA court is the same shape as the lane on an NCAA court, are they congruent? Explain.

_____

_____

3. The lane on a WNBA court is 12 feet by 19 feet. If the lane is the same shape as that of the NBA lane, are they congruent? Why or why not?

_____

_____

Choose the letter for the best answer.

4. The parallelograms below are congruent. What is the measure of $\angle U$?

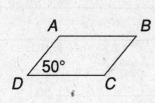 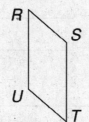

   A 50°   C 100°

   B 130°   D 260°

6. In $\triangle ABC$, $m\angle A = m\angle B$, and $m\angle C = 100°$. What are the measures of the angles in $\triangle DEF$ if it is congruent to $\triangle ABC$?

   A 60°, 60°, 100°

   B 20°, 60°, 100°

   C 30°, 60°, 100°

   D 40°, 40°, 100°

5. The Mexican flag is a rectangle divided into three vertical stripes of identical measures. Which of the following statements is true about the Mexican flag?

   F It has 3 congruent rectangles.

   G It has 3 rectangles that are not congruent.

   H It has 4 congruent rectangles.

   J It has 4 rectangles and none are congruent.

7. $\triangle JKL$ is congruent to $\triangle RST$. $\angle L$ and $\angle T$ are right angles. Which statement about the two triangles is *not* true?

   F $m\angle K = m\angle S$

   G $\overline{JK} \cong \overline{RS}$

   H $m\angle J = m\angle L$

   J $m\angle R + m\angle S = 90°$

Holt McDougal Mathematics

Name _____ Date _____ Class _____

Write the correct answer.

Clock 1

Clock 2

1. If you reflect the hands of clock 1 across a line from 12 to 6, what time will it show?

_____

2. If you rotate the hour hand on clock 2 by 90° clockwise, what time will it be?

_____

3. The hands on clock 1 show 7:00 after a transformation of one hand. What was the transformation?

_____

_____

4. The hands on clock 2 show 9:00 after a transformation. Name 2 different transformations that could produce this change.

_____

_____

_____

Choose the letter for the best answer.

5. What transformation of triangle 1 created triangle 2?

   A translation 3 units right and 1 unit down

   B translation 8 units right and 1 unit down

   C rotation of 180° about the origin

   D reflection across the y-axis

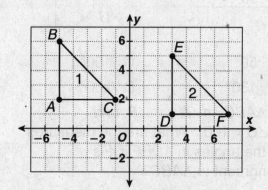

6. If you rotate triangle 2 90° clockwise about vertex D, what will be the coordinates of the new triangle?

   F $D'(3, 1), E'(7, 1), F'(3, -3)$

   G $D'(3, 1), E'(3, -3), F'(7, 1)$

   H $D'(3, 1), E'(-4, 1), F'(-3, 3)$

   J $D'(3, 1), E'(-3, 3), F'(-7, 1)$

7. If you reflect triangle 1 across the x-axis, what will be the coordinates of the new triangle?

   A $A'(5, 2), B'(5, 6), C'(1, 2)$

   B $A'(-5, 0), B'(-5, -4), C'(-1, 0)$

   C $A'(5, -2), B'(5, -6), C'(1, -2)$

   D $A'(-5, -2), B'(-5, -6), C'(-1, -2)$

Holt McDougal Mathematics

Problem Solving

LESSON 8-11

Symmetry

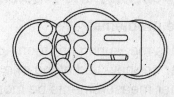

Write the correct answer.

Use the logo of an Australian TV station for Exercises 1 and 2.

1. How many lines of symmetry do the dots in the Channel 9 logo have?

   _____

   _____

2. How many times will the dots show rotational symmetry in 1 rotation of 360°? What is the smallest angle of rotational symmetry for the dots?

   _____

3. The figure on an emblem will show rotational symmetry 8 times within a single rotation. What is the smallest angle of rotational symmetry for the emblem?

   _____

4. Draw a figure that shows rotational symmetry 5 times within a 360° rotation.

Choose the letter for the best answer.

5. Which is a true statement about the stained glass window?

   A It is asymmetrical.

   B It has 1 line of symmetry.

   C It will show rotational symmetry 4 times within a full rotation.

   D It has 2 lines of symmetry.

6. Which is a true statement about the time shown on the clocks?

3:08	4:00	6:13	1:30
1	2	3	4

   F Only clocks 1 and 2 have a line of symmetry.

   G All of the clocks have at least 1 line of symmetry.

   H All of the clocks are asymmetrical.

   J Only clocks 1 and 4 have a line of symmetry.

Holt McDougal Mathematics

LESSON 9-1 Problem Solving
Accuracy and Precision

Solve the problems.

1. Carol is measuring her room to center her new bed along one wall. Will her measurements be more precise if she uses centimeters or inches? Explain.

_____

_____

2. Normal rainfall in Hilo, Hawaii is 2.36 feet per year. Yearly, rainfall in Honolulu, Hawaii is 7.77 inches. Which measurement is more precise? Explain.

_____

_____

3. The Akashi-Kaikyo Bridge in Japan measures 6,529 feet. The Great Belt Bridge in Denmark measures 1,624 m. Which measurement is more precise? Explain.

_____

_____

4. Santa Barbara, California, gets an average of 1.03 feet of rainfall every year. The city of Santa Maria gets 13.95 inches. Which measurement is more precise? Explain.

_____

_____

The drawing shows salad dressing ingredients. The top liquid is oil, the bottom vinegar. Circle the correct answer.

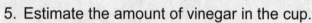

5. Estimate the amount of vinegar in the cup.

   A. $2\frac{1}{2}$ fl oz   C. $3\frac{1}{2}$ fl oz

   B. 3 fl oz   D. 4 fl oz

6. Estimate the amount of oil in the cup.

   A. $\frac{3}{4}$ fl oz   C. $3\frac{3}{4}$ fl oz

   B. $\frac{2}{3}$ fl oz   D. 4 fl oz

7. Estimate the amount of water it would take to fill the cup to the 6-oz level.

   A. $1\frac{1}{4}$ fl oz   C. 3 fl oz

   B. $2\frac{1}{4}$ fl oz   D. $6\frac{3}{4}$ fl oz

Holt Mathematics

Problem Solving

LESSON 9-2

Perimeter and Circumference

Write the correct answer.

1. Mr. Marcos, the gym teacher, had the seventh graders run around the perimeter of the gym 3 times. The gym has a length of 34 feet and a width of 58 feet. What was the total distance the students ran?

2. The distance between bases on a baseball field is 90 feet. If 3 players hit home runs during a game and each runs around all 4 bases, what is the total distance the players run?

3. Basketball rims have a diameter of 18 inches. If you want to put a band around a basketball rim, how much material to the nearest tenth of an inch will you need?

4. A pizza cutter has a diameter of 2.5 inches. To cut a pizza in half, the cutter makes two complete revolutions. What is the diameter of the pizza?

5. A round stained-glass window has a circumference of 195 inches. What is the radius of the window to the nearest inch?

6. A planter full of pansies has a diameter of 14 inches. What is the circumference of the planter to the nearest inch?

Choose the letter of the correct answer.

7. A welcome mat on the front porch is a semicircle. The straight side of the mat is 36 inches. What is the perimeter of the mat?
   A 92.52 in.   C 56.52 in.
   B 64.26 in.   D 28.26 in.

8. The radius of the planet Jupiter is about 44,368 miles. What is the approximate circumference of Jupiter to the nearest mile?
   F 557,262 mi   H 139,316 mi
   G 278,631 mi   J 69,658 mi

9. Four square tables with sides of 48 inches each are placed end to end to form one big table. What is the perimeter of the table that is formed?
   A 192 in.   C 480 in.
   B 384 in.   D 768 in.

10. The Great Pyramid at Giza, Egypt, has a base with four equal sides. If the perimeter of the pyramid is 3,023 feet, what is the length (to the nearest foot) of one side of the base of the pyramid?
    F 754 ft   H 756 ft
    G 755 ft   J 757 ft

Holt Mathematics

Problem Solving

LESSON 9-3

Area of Parallelograms

Write the correct answer.

1. A dollar bill has an area of 15.86 square inches. If a dollar bill is 2.6 inches long, how wide is it?

_____

2. On an official United States flag, the ratio of width to length is exactly 1 to 1.9. What is the area of a United States flag whose width is 2 feet?

_____

3. A back yard is shaped like a parallelogram with a height of 32 feet and a base of 100 feet. One bag of grass seed covers 125 square feet. What is the least number of bags of seed needed to seed the lawn?

_____

4. The art club is painting a mural on a school wall. The mural is in the shape of a parallelogram. If the base of the mural is 10.5 feet long and the mural covers 89.25 square feet, how high is the mural?

_____

Choose the letter of the correct answer.

5. In baseball, the area of each base is 225 square inches. Each base is a square. What is the length of each side of a base on a baseball field?

   A 12 in.   C 25 in.

   B 22.5 in.   D 15 in.

6. The area of a parallelogram is 632.1 square centimeters. Its base is 24.5 centimeters. What is the height of the parallelogram?

   F 25.8 cm   H 21.9 cm

   G 705.6 cm   J 11.8 cm

7. The official rules for volleyball were developed in 1897. The rules state that the court or floor space must be 25 feet wide and 50 feet long. An official basketball court is 94 feet by 50 feet. How much larger is the area of a basketball court than the area of a volleyball court?

   A 69 ft^2 larger

   B 3,450 ft^2 larger

   C 1,250 ft^2 larger

   D 4,700 ft^2 larger

8. Two parallelograms each have an area of 288 square inches. One has a height of 12 inches, and the other has a height of 18 inches. What are the bases of each parallelogram?

   F 40 in. and 30 in.

   G 22 in. and 15 in.

   H 24 in. and 16 in.

   J 26 in. and 20 in.

Holt Mathematics

LESSON
9-4

Problem Solving

Area of Triangles and Trapezoids

Write the correct answer.

The diagram shows the dimensions of the sails on a model sailboat. Use the diagram to solve Problems 1–2.

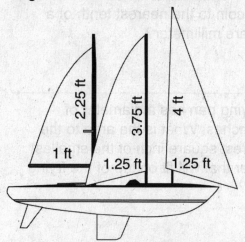

1. About how much material to the nearest square foot will be needed to make the sails?

_____

2. If the dimensions for each sail were doubled, how would that change the total amount of material needed to make the sails?

_____

_____

3. A flower bed is shaped like a trapezoid with a height of 3.5 yards, one 2.8-yard base, and another 4.6-yard base. A packet of flower seeds covers 5.6 square yards. What is the least number of packets needed to plant the flower bed?

_____

4. A triangular road sign has a height of 8 feet and a base of 16.5 feet. How much larger in area is this sign than one with a height of 4 feet and a base of 8.25 feet?

_____

Choose the letter of the correct answer.

This diagram shows the top view of the roof of a house.

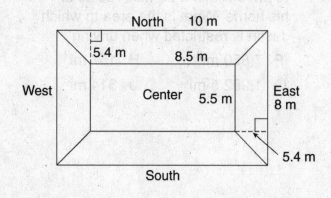

5. If you need to reshingle the north and south sections of the roof, how many square meters of shingles will you need?

   A 199.8 m^2 C 49.95 m^2

   B 99.9 m^2 D 459 m^2

6. If you need to reshingle the west section of the roof, how many square meters of shingles will you need?

   F 13.5 m^2 H 36.45 m^2

   G 18.9 m^2 J 72.9 m^2

Holt Mathematics

LESSON
9-5

Problem Solving

Area of Circles

Write the correct answer.

1. According to the Royal Canadian Mint Act, a 50-cent Canadian coin must have a diameter of 27.13 millimeters. What is the area of this coin to the nearest tenth of a square millimeter?

2. By regulation, the diameter of a 25-cent Canadian coin is 23.88 millimeters. What is the area of this coin to the nearest tenth of a square millimeter?

3. There is a water reservoir beneath a circular garden to supply a fountain in the garden. The reservoir has a 26-inch diameter. The garden has a 12-foot diameter. How much of the garden does not contain the water reservoir?

4. A frying pan has a diameter of 11 inches. What is the area to the nearest square inch of the smallest cover that will fit on top of the frying pan?

Choose the letter of the correct answer.

5. In the state of Texas, Austin is about 80 miles northeast of San Antonio. What area is represented by all of the land within 80 miles of San Antonio?

   A 251.2 mi^2 C 5,024 mi^2

   B 502.4 mi^2 D 20,096 mi^2

6. A standard CD has a diameter of 12 centimeters. What is the area of a circular case that can be used to store a CD?

   F 114 cm^2 H 105 cm^2

   G 112 cm^2 J 92 cm^2

7. A round dining table has a diameter of 2.5 meters. A round tablecloth has a diameter of 3.5 meters. What is the area to the nearest tenth of a meter of the part of the tablecloth that will hang down the side of the table?

   A 18.8 m^2 C 4.7 m^2

   B 6.3 m^2 D 1.0 m^2

8. Justin just got his driver's license. His parents are giving him permission to drive within a 25-mile radius of his home. What is the area to which Justin is restricted when driving?

   F 7,850 mi^2 H 157 mi^2

   G 1,962.5 mi^2 J 314 mi^2

LESSON 9-6

Problem Solving
Area of Irregular Figures

Write the correct answer.

1. Explain how to find the area of the composite figure below. Then find the area.

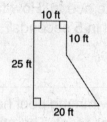

10 ft

10 ft

25 ft

20 ft

_____

_____

2. Mr. Bemis carpets the living room shown below. If he pays $20 per square meter, what is the total cost of the carpet?

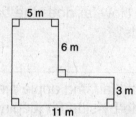

5 m

6 m

3 m

11 m

_____

3. A figure is made of a square and a semi-circle. The square has sides of 16 cm each. One side of the square is also the diameter of the semi-circle. What is the total area of the figure? Use 3.14 for π.

_____

4. A figure is made of a rectangle and an isosceles right triangle. The rectangle has sides of 6 in. and 3 in. One of the short sides of the rectangle is also one of the legs of the right triangle. What is the total area of the figure?

_____

Choose the letter of the correct answer.

5. Norene builds the deck at the right. The area of the deck is 10 m^2 greater than was originally planned. What is the area of the deck?

   A 110 m^2 C 66 m^2

   B 76 m^2 D 56 m^2

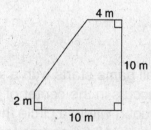

4 m

10 m

2 m

10 m

6. The grid to the right shows a swimming pool. Each square represents 1 square meter. What is the best estimate of the area of the swimming pool?

   F 45 m^2 H 37 m^2

   G 41 m^2 J 32 m^2

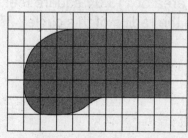

Holt McDougal Mathematics

Problem Solving

LESSON 9-7

Squares and Square Roots

Write the correct answer. For Problems 1 and 2, use the following formula to find the distance in meters a free-falling object falls from a place of rest: $d = 0.5 \cdot 9.8 \cdot t^2$ (t = time in seconds).

1. As part of a science experiment, Hsing drops a ball from the roof of the school. How far does the ball fall in 2 seconds?

2. Mel drops a stone from the edge of a cliff overlooking the ocean. How far does the stone fall in 5 seconds?

3. At the county fair, the apple pies are lined up side-by-side for judging along the length of a 6-foot table. Each pie has an area of 50.24 in². How many pies are on the table?

4. The community swimming pool has an area of 1,024 square feet. The pool is in the shape of a square. What is the perimeter of the pool?

Choose the letter of the correct answer.

5. The Portuguese national flag is a rectangle. In the center of the flag is a coat of arms and shield on a circle. This circle has a diameter that is half the flag's height. If the flag's circle has an area of 3.14 square feet, what is the height of the flag?

   A 1 ft

   B 3 ft

   C 4 ft

   D 2 ft

6. A square picture has an area of 81 square inches. The perimeter of the frame for the picture is 8 inches longer than the perimeter of the picture itself. What is the length of each side of the square frame for this picture?

   F 8 in.

   G 10 in.

   H 9 in.

   J 11 in.

7. A basketball game starts with a jump ball. This occurs in the center of the basketball court within a circle that has an area of 113.04 square feet. What is the radius of this circle?

   A 3 ft

   B 6 ft

   C 9 ft

   D 36 ft

8. A square fence encloses a vegetable garden with an area of 169 square feet. What is the perimeter of the fence?

   F 52 ft

   G 26 ft

   H 13 ft

   J 56.25 ft

Problem Solving

The Pythagorean Theorem

Write the correct answer.

1. During a storm, a tree falls toward a house. The top of the tree leans against the house 45 feet above the ground. The distance on the ground from the house to the base of the tree is 24 feet. What is the height of the tree?

   _____

2. During a training exercise, a firefighter leans a 40-foot ladder up to a window in a house. The bottom of the ladder is 24 feet from the bottom of the house. How high is the window from the ground?

   _____

3. A triangle has a hypotenuse of 25 centimeters and a base of 20 centimeters. What is the area of this right triangle?

   _____

4. The football field at the University of Texas at Arlington is 60 yards by 100 yards. Is the length of the diagonal across this field more or less than 200 yards? Explain.

   _____

   _____

Choose the letter of the correct answer.

5. The minimum size of a soccer field for players under 8 years of age is 20 yards by 30 yards. About how far is the diagonal distance on a field with these dimensions?

   A about 12 yd   C about 36 yd

   B about 25 yd   D about 45 yd

6. The minimum size of a soccer field for international matches is 70 yards by 110 yards. If a player runs diagonally across this field, about how much farther does she run than if the field were 50 yards by 100 yards?

   F about 242 yd   H about 112 yd

   G about 130 yd   J about 19 yd

7. In the state of Virginia, Winchester is 21 miles north of Front Royal. Arlington is 58 miles east of Front Royal. What is the distance to the nearest mile from Winchester to Arlington?

   A 37 mi   C 89 mi

   B 62 mi   D 441 mi

8. On a child's slide, the distance from the bottom rung to the top of the ladder is 6 feet. The straight distance from the bottom rung of the ladder to the bottom of the slide is 36 inches. About how long is the slide?

   F about 6.7 ft   H about 9.0 ft

   G about 8.4 ft   J about 36.5 ft

Holt McDougal Mathematics

LESSON 10-1 — Problem Solving
Introduction to Three-Dimensional Figures

Write the correct answer.

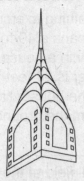

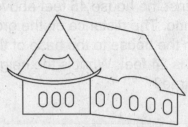

1. The picture above shows the top of the Chrysler Building in New York City. It was completed in 1930. Does the top of the tower most resemble a prism or a pyramid? Explain.

_____

_____

_____

2. The picture above shows the rooftop of Himeji Castle, completed in 1614 in Donjon, Himeji City, Japan. Do the rooftops resemble pyramids or prisms? Explain.

_____

_____

_____

3. An architect designed a structure for the top of building. The structure has a vertex, one circular base, and a curved surface. What three-dimensional figure is it?

_____

4. On a farm, grain is stored in a silo. This is a very tall structure with a circular base and top and a curved surface. What three-dimensional figure does it resemble?

_____

Choose the letter of the correct answer.

5. James put two blocks together to build the figure shown. Identify the two figures he used.

  A two pyramids

  B a pyramid and a prism

  C a pyramid and a cone

  D two prisms

6. Jaime constructs a figure that has one rectangular base and four triangular faces. What is the figure?

  F a cone

  G a triangular pyramid

  H a rectangular pyramid

  J a rectangular prism

7. The shape of a log is most like which figure?

  A cylinder   C prism

  B pyramid   D cone

LESSON	**Problem Solving**
10-2	*Volume of Prisms and Cylinders*

Write the correct answer.

1. The eight Corinthian columns at the National Building Museum in Washington, DC, are each 75 feet high and 8 feet in diameter. What is the volume of each column?

2. A cubic centimeter holds 1 milliliter of liquid. How many liters of water to the nearest tenth are required to fill a fish tank that is 24 centimeters high, 28 centimeters long, and 36 centimeters wide?

3. There are 231 cubic inches in a gallon. A large juice can has a diameter of 6 inches and a height of 10 inches. How many gallons of juice does the can hold? Round your answer to the nearest tenth.

4. A small gift box that holds a ring is shaped like a cube. The box measures 1.4 inches on each side. What is the volume of the gift box? Round your answer to the nearest tenth.

Choose the letter of the correct answer.

5. The Leaning Tower of Pisa in Italy appears to be cylindrical in shape. Its height is about 56 meters. If the volume of the tower is about 9,891 cubic meters, what is the diameter of the base?

   A about 3.5 m   C about 15 m

   B about 7 m   D about 20 m

6. A bricklayer is building a brick rectangular post to anchor a mailbox. The post is 3 feet tall, 2 feet deep, and 2 feet wide. Each brick is 3 inches by 6 inches by 3 inches. How many bricks does he need?

   F 12 bricks   H 197 bricks

   G 54 bricks   J 384 bricks

7. The average stone on the lowest level of the Great Pyramid in Egypt was a rectangular prism 5 feet long by 5 feet high by 6 feet deep and weighed 15 tons. What was the volume of the average stone?

   A 1,800 ft^3 C 150 ft^3

   B 1,800 ft^2 D 150 ft^2

8. A cylindrical barrel is 2.8 feet in diameter and 8 feet high. If a cubic foot holds about 7.5 gallons of liquid, how many gallons of water will this barrel hold?

   F about 1,477 gal

   G about 369 gal

   H about 150 gal

   J about 470 gal

         Holt McDougal Mathematics

Problem Solving

LESSON 10-3

Volume of Pyramids and Cones

Write the correct answer.

1. Each of the cone-shaped cups near the water cooler has a radius of 3 centimeters and a height of 10 centimeters. If 1 cubic centimeter can hold 1 milliliter of liquid, how much water can each cup hold?

_____

2. The Great Pyramid in Egypt has a square base that measures 751 feet on each side. The pyramid is 481 feet high. What is the volume of the Great Pyramid? Round your answer to the nearest cubic foot.

_____

3. A waffle cone that holds ice cream is 15 centimeters high and has a diameter of 10 centimeters. What volume of ice cream can it hold if it is filled to the top?

_____

4. The base of a rectangular prism is congruent to the base of a pyramid. The height of the pyramid is 3 times the height of the prism. Which figure has a greater volume? Explain.

_____

_____

_____

Choose the letter of the correct answer.

5. A teepee that is shaped like a cone has a diameter of 12 feet and a height of 15 feet. What is the volume of the teepee?

A 565.2 ft³   C 1,695.6 ft³

B 706.5 ft³   D 2,119.5 ft³

6. The top of a 44-story office building is shaped like a pyramid. The base of the pyramid is a right triangle with the two legs measuring 73 feet and 78 feet. The pyramid is 35 feet high. What is the volume of the pyramid?

F 199,290 ft³   H 41,756 ft³

G 66,430 ft³   J 33,215 ft³

7. The diameter of a cone-shaped container is 4 inches. Its height is 6 inches. How much greater is the volume of a cylinder-shaped container with the same diameter and height?

A 50.24 in³   C 100.98 in³

B 75.36 in³   D 200.96 in³

8. A square pyramid mold for a candle has a base of 64 square centimeters and a height of 12 centimeters. How much greater is the volume of a rectangular prism mold with the same base and height?

F 64 cm³   H 256 cm³

G 96 cm³   J 512 cm³

Holt McDougal Mathematics

Problem Solving

LESSON 10-4

Surface Area of Prisms and Cylinders

Write the correct answer.

1. A can of peas is 3 inches in diameter and 4.5 inches tall. What is the area of the label used around the can?

   _____

2. How much wrapping paper do you need to completely cover a rectangular box that is 20 inches by 18 inches by 2 inches?

   _____

3. Jan puts frosting on a circular cake. The cake has three layers, each with a diameter of 20 centimeters and a height of 5 centimeters. Jan puts frosting between the layers and on the outside, except for the bottom. What is the area that Jan frosts? Round to the nearest square centimeter.

   _____

4. A cardboard storage carton has a length of 3 feet, a width of 2 feet, and a volume of 12 ft^3. What is the minimum amount of cardboard needed to make the box?

   _____

Choose the letter of the correct answer.

5. A cylindrical building is 30 meters in diameter and 50 meters high. The outside of the building, excluding the roof, is completely covered in glass. To the nearest square foot, what is the total area of the glass?

   A 1,413 m^3 C 6,113 m^3

   B 4,710 m^3 D 9,420 m^3

6. Rebecca gives gifts to 12 employees. Each gift is in a box that is 12 inches by 10 inches by 3 inches. How much wrapping paper does Rebecca need to completely the cover the boxes?

   F 360 in^2 H 4,464 in^2

   G 1,720 in^2 J 14,400 in^2

7. A cylinder-shaped sculpture is 24 meters high with a diameter of 6.8 meters. An artist plans to spray-paint the entire surface with silver paint. If one can of spray paint covers 50 square meters, how many cans does the artist need to paint the sculpture?

   A 51 cans   C 12 cans

   B 22 cans   D 10 cans

8. A rectangular sofa cushion is 36 inches by 30 inches by 20 inches. How many cushions can be covered with 38,400 square inches of material?

   F 6 cushions   H 39 cushions

   G 8 cushions   J 10 cushions

Holt McDougal Mathematics

LESSON
10-5

Problem Solving

Surface Area of Pyramids and Cones

Solve the problems.

1. A three-sided pyramid and square pyramid both have a base perimeter of 30 cm and the same slant height and surface area. What is the base height of the three-sided pyramid?

_____

_____

2. The surface area of a cone is exactly 4,396 units^2. The radius of the circular base is $\frac{2}{5}$ the slant height of the cone. Find r and ℓ. Use 3.14 for π.

_____

_____

3. The Ladrones Tower in Marbella, Spain, is a cone-shaped building with a base circumference of 12 m and a slant height of 14.7 m. Find the surface area of the structure. *Hint*: The formula $\frac{C}{d} = \pi$ expresses the relationship between the circumference and diameter of a circle.

_____

_____

4. The Transamerica Building in San Francisco is a square pyramid with a metal top. The metal top has a base perimeter of 43 m and a slant height of 65 m. How many square meters of aluminum were required for the top of the Transamerica Building?

_____

_____

_____

At the right is a square pyramid designed by Chinese-American architect I.M. Pei. Use it to answer the questions. Circle the letter of the correct answer.

5. The pyramid's base area is

  A 35 m

  B 140 m^2

  C 1,225 m^2

  D 122 m

6. The surface area is of the glass walls is

  A 1,890 m^2

  B 2,112 m^2

  C 4,114 m^2

  D 6,028 m^2

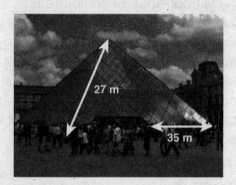

Holt McDougal Mathematics

Problem Solving

LESSON 10-6

Changing Dimensions

Write the correct answer.

1. In the late 1800s, wax cylinders were used to record sound. The surface area of the curved side of each cylinder was about 25 square inches. If a larger model of this cylinder is created using a scale factor of 3, what is the lateral surface area of the model?

2. A 5-foot wide, 100-foot tall cylindrical water tower was built in St. Louis in the early 1800s. An architecture student wants to build a model using a scale factor of $\frac{1}{6}$. What will be the volume of the model to the nearest cubic foot?

3. A cone-shaped plastic cup holds 24 ounces of water. A smaller cup has a scale factor of $\frac{1}{2}$. How much water does the smaller cup hold?

4. In the game of Ring Taw, players use a shooting marble that has a surface area of 1.77 square inches. What is the surface area of a large ball if the scale factor is 5?

Choose the letter of the correct answer.

5. The volume of a rectangular prism is 48 cubic centimeters. The volume of a similar rectangular prism is 6 cubic centimeters What is the scale factor for the rectangles?

   A 8

   B 6

   C 4

   D 2

6. A cooking pot used in the cafeteria weighs 64 pounds when it is filled with soup. How much would a similar pot with a scale factor of $\frac{1}{2}$ weigh when filled with the same soup?

   F 4 lb   H 16 lb

   G 8 lb   J 32 lb

7. For his science project, Marty is building a model of Pluto, which has a surface area of about 6,376,000 square miles. He plans to cover his model with red foil. If he uses a scale factor of 5,000, how much red foil will he need to the nearest hundredth of a square mile?

   A 1.26 mi²   C 0.26 mi²

   B 0.026 mi²   D 0.126 mi²

8. The scale factor of two similar triangular prisms is 5. What is the possible surface area of both prisms?

   F 2,000 cm² and 80 cm²

   G 125 cm² and 25 cm²

   H 5,000 cm² and 40 cm²

   J 10,000 cm² and 60 cm²

Holt McDougal Mathematics

LESSON
11-1

Problem Solving
Probability

Write the correct answer.

1. Of the original 56 signers of the Declaration of Independence, four of them represented North Carolina. If you selected one signer randomly, how likely is it that he represented North Carolina?

2. One question on a social studies multiple-choice test has four possible answers. Marianne is sure two of the choices are incorrect. How likely is she to choose the correct answer?

3. There are 8 right-handed pitchers and 2 left-handed pitchers on the Tigers baseball team. How likely is it that their opponents will face a right-handed pitcher?

4. Every seventh-grade student is attending a presentation about recycling in the auditorium. Jaleel is a seventh-grade student. How likely is it that he is in the auditorium?

Choose the letter for the best answer.

The table shows the contents of Leticia's CD and DVD collection.

5. How likely is it that a disk chosen randomly is a CD?

   A unlikely   C certain

   B as likely as not   D likely

6. How likely is it that a disk chosen randomly is a jazz CD?

   F unlikely   H likely

   G as likely as not   J impossible

7. Sally picks a disk at random from Leticia's collection. How likely is it that it is a comedy DVD?

   A as likely as not

   B likely

   C certain

   D unlikely

Leticia's CD and DVD Collection

Type of CD/DVD	Number
Rock CD	26
Pop CD	17
Comedy DVD	11
Drama DVD	2

8. Leticia picks three disks from her collection at random. Which outcome is impossible?

   F They are all rock CDs.

   G They are all drama DVDs.

   H None of them are rock CDs.

   J They are all DVDs.

Holt McDougal Mathematics

LESSON	**Problem Solving**
11-2	*Experimental Probability*

Write the correct answer as a fraction in simplest form.

This table shows a breakdown by format of total music sales in the United States in 2004.

Total American Music Sales in 2004

Format	Total (% of units shipped)
CD	80
Digital Single	15
Music Video	3
Other	2

1. What is the experimental probability that any random music purchase in 2004 was a CD?

_____

2. What is the experimental probability that any random music purchase in 2004 was not a Music Video?

_____

3. What is the experimental probability that any random music purchase in 2004 was a digital single?

_____

4. Which combination of sales has an experimental probability of $\frac{1}{20}$?

_____

Choose the letter for the best answer.

5. Ethan hits 4 ringers in 10 attempts while pitching horseshoes. What does an experimental probability of $\frac{2}{5}$ describe?

   A P(horseshoes)

   B P(missed shots)

   C P(attempts)

   D P(ringers)

6. Jay beats Terry at table tennis 3 out of 5 games. What is the experimental probability that Terry will win their next game?

   F $\frac{1}{2}$ H $\frac{2}{5}$

   G $\frac{3}{5}$ J 1

7. Poonam counts 10 classmates out of 36 people in the library. What is the experimental probability that the next person will be a classmate?

   A $\frac{5}{36}$ C $\frac{1}{36}$

   B $\frac{5}{18}$ D $\frac{1}{10}$

8. Macy makes 15 of 20 free throws at basketball practice. What is the experimental probability that she will miss her next free throw?

   F $\frac{1}{4}$ H $\frac{2}{3}$

   G $\frac{1}{2}$ J $\frac{3}{4}$

LESSON 11-3	**Problem Solving**
	Sample Spaces

Write the correct answer.

1. If you order one topping, how many different choices of bagel and toppings can you order?

_____

2. Santana only likes cream cheese or jam on his bagel. How many choices does he have for a one-topping bagel?

_____

3. Yesterday, Benny ran out of raisin bagels. How many choices of a bagel and one topping were there?

_____

4. Today, Benny has all 5 types of bagels but runs out of honey. How many choices of a bagel with one topping can you order?

_____

Benny's Bagels

Bagels	Toppings
Plain	Cream cheese
Poppy	Honey
Raisin	Butter
Sesame	Jam
Egg	

Choose the letter for the best answer.

5. The mall movie multiplex is showing 12 movies. Each movie is shown at five different times during the day. How many choices of movies and showtimes does Reggie have?

A 5　　　　　C 17

B 12　　　　 D 60

6. At Hi-Top Ski Resort, there are three chair lifts to the top of the mountain. There are six ski trails to the bottom of the mountain. How many possible choices of lifts and trails do the skiers have?

F 9　　　　　H 81

G 18　　　　 J 2

7. In a Little League game, Geri can bat first, second, or third. When at bat, she could strike out, walk, or get a hit. How many outcomes are in the sample space for these events?

A 3

B 6

C 9

D 18

8. Ty is flipping a coin. He has decided that if he flips the same result twice in a row, he will do his homework. If he flips 2 different results, then he will go jogging. How likely is it that he will study?

F as likely as not

G likely

H unlikely

J certain

Holt McDougal Mathematics

LESSON 11-4	**Problem Solving**
	Theoretical Probability

Write the correct answer in simplest form.

The table lists the pieces used in the game of chess.

Chess Set

Type	White	Black
Pawn	8	8
Rook	2	2
Knight	2	2
Bishop	2	2
Queen	1	1
King	1	1

1. If you randomly choose a piece of the chess set, what is the probability that it is a pawn? Write your answer as a decimal.

_____

2. If you randomly choose a piece of the chess set, what is the probability that it is a white pawn? Write your answer as a decimal.

_____

3. If you randomly choose a piece of the chess set, what is the probability that it is a rook, knight, or bishop? Write your answer as a fraction.

_____

4. If you randomly choose a piece of the chess set, what is the probability that it is a queen? Write your answer as a fraction.

_____

Choose the letter for the best answer.

5. Mr. Rose randomly selects names to see who will give the first book report. There are 10 boys and 14 girls in his class. What is the probability that he will select a girl's name?

A $\frac{2}{5}$ C $\frac{7}{12}$

B $\frac{5}{12}$ D $\frac{5}{7}$

6. Eight students will give reports on novels, 9 will report on biographies, and 7 will report on history books. What is the probability that the first report will be a novel?

F $\frac{3}{8}$ H $\frac{8}{17}$

G $\frac{1}{3}$ J $\frac{1}{2}$

7. Stanley is reading a 224-page book. There are illustrations on 14 pages. If Stanley opens the book at random, what is the probability that the page will have an illustration?

A 0.0004   C 0.0714

B 0.0625   D 0.9375

8. In Congress, each of the 50 states is represented by 2 senators. If you choose a senator randomly, what is the probability that you will choose a senator that represents Virginia?

F 25%   H 2%

G 10%   J 1%

Holt McDougal Mathematics

LESSON
11-5

Problem Solving

Making Predictions

Solve the problems.

1. An ad for the new elevated train line states that it is on time 96% of the time. The subway, which Bob has been taking, has been on time 79 times out of 83. Should Bob switch to the elevated train? Why or why not?

_____

_____

2. The school picnic, which is a two-day weekend event, has been scheduled for April this year. The area routinely gets 16 rainy days in April. Do the planners have a better than even chance of choosing a dry weekend during April? Explain.

_____

_____

3. The Hirsch family is planning a three-week trip to the rainforest this August. This area experiences humidity levels of 90% or more 70% of the time in August. How many days in the rainforest can the family expect to have humidity levels below 90%? Explain.

_____

_____

4. Postal Xpress has been late delivering packages only 1 time in every 28 deliveries. Lightning Overnite, a new company, claims it will beat Postal Xpress's record.
What percentage of its deliveries will the new company have to make on-time? Explain.

_____

_____

The blue space on the spinner equals half the area. Of the remaining area, two thirds are green. Use the spinner to answer questions 5–8. Circle the letter of the correct answer.

5. How many spins out of 80 are likely to be blue?

   A 30   C 50

   B 40   D none of the above

6. How many spins out of 80 are likely to be green?

   A about 6   C about 13

   B about 8   D about 27

7. How many spins out of 650 are likely to be either red or green?

   A 246   C about 309

   B about 290   D 325

Holt McDougal Mathematics

LESSON 11-6

Problem Solving

Probability of Independent and Dependent Events

Write the correct answer.

1. Li rolls a pair of number cubes twice. On both rolls, the sum is 7. Are the rolls dependent or independent events?

2. Nine boys and 12 girls want to play soccer. Teams are formed by selecting one player at a time. Is the probability of selecting a boy after a girl is selected a dependent or an independent event?

3. Gregg has 12 cards. Half are black, and half are red. He picks two cards out of the deck. What is the probability that both cards are red?

4. In basketball, Alan makes 1 out of every 4 free throws he attempts. What is the probability that Alan will make his next 3 free throws?

Choose the letter for the best answer.

5. There are 8 blue marbles and 7 red marbles in a bag. Julie pulls two marbles at random from the bag first. What is the probability that she first pulls a blue marble and then a red marble?

   A $\frac{8}{15}$ C $\frac{4}{7}$

   B $\frac{4}{15}$ D $\frac{1}{2}$

6. You roll a 1–6 number cube twice. What is the probability that you roll a 3 on the first roll and a 6 on the second roll?

   F $\frac{1}{36}$ H $\frac{1}{6}$

   G $\frac{1}{9}$ J $\frac{1}{2}$

7. Andrew has $2.00 in quarters in his pocket, including three state quarters. He takes two quarters out of his pocket. What is the probability that they are **not** state quarters?

   A $\frac{3}{8}$ C $\frac{3}{14}$

   B $\frac{5}{8}$ D $\frac{5}{14}$

8. Jamie has 3 raffle tickets. One hundred tickets were sold. Her name was not drawn for the first prize. What is the probability that her name will be drawn for the second prize?

   F $\frac{1}{3}$ H $\frac{1}{33}$

   G $\frac{3}{100}$ J $\frac{2}{99}$

Holt McDougal Mathematics

LESSON 11-7 Problem Solving
Combinations

Write the correct answer.

1. Six friends are going to play a ball game. Each team has 3 players. How many different team combinations are possible?

_____

2. Yung wants to visit 3 of the 5 Great Lakes this summer. How many different combinations of lakes are possible?

_____

3. There are 4 spots left for a school field trip. Roberta, Samuel, Thea, Ling, Jose, and Mark all want to go on the trip. How many different combinations are possible for the remaining 4 spots?

_____

4. At summer camp, the campers pick two activities for the first day of camp. They can choose from among hiking, canoeing, rock climbing, and bird watching. How many different combinations of activities are there?

_____

Choose the letter for the best answer.

5. Eight children are playing a trivia game. They want to make teams of 2 players each. How many different team combinations are possible?

   A 10 combinations

   B 21 combinations

   C 28 combinations

   D 56 combinations

6. At Washington Middle School, a student takes 4 core classes a day. There are 6 different core classes offered. How many different combinations of classes are there?

   F 10 combinations

   G 12 combinations

   H 15 combinations

   J 24 combinations

7. The class is drawing maps of the 7 continents to display in the school lobby. The main wall in the lobby has room for 3 maps. How many combinations of maps are possible for that location?

   A 10 combinations

   B 21 combinations

   C 30 combinations

   D 35 combinations

8. Ms. Henrie's literature class is voting on the 2 most influential people of the eighteenth century. The choices are 5 famous people. How many different combinations are possible?

   F 7 combinations

   G 8 combinations

   H 10 combinations

   J 15 combinations

Problem Solving

LESSON
11-8

Permutations

Write the correct answer.

1. Five snowboarders are competing in a half-pipe competition during the Winter Sports Festival. In how many different orders can the snowboarders compete?

   _____

2. In how many different orders can, Debbie, Brigitte, and Adam wait in line in the school cafeteria? What is the probability that they will be in alphabetical order?

   _____

3. In how many different orders can the science class study the planets Jupiter, Saturn, Uranus, and Neptune? What is the probability that they will study Saturn first?

   _____

4. The physical education teacher sets up 8 different exercise stations for the class to complete. In how many different orders can the stations be done?

   _____

Choose the letter for the best answer.

5. Hannah, Javier, and Beth were the three qualifiers for a race. In how many different orders can they finish? What is the probability that Hannah or Beth will be first?

   A 3 orders; $\frac{1}{3}$ C 6 orders; $\frac{1}{3}$

   B 3 orders; $\frac{2}{3}$ D 6 orders; $\frac{2}{3}$

6. Berto and 5 friends have ordered dinner at a restaurant. What is the probability that Berto will be served last?

   F $\frac{1}{720}$ H $\frac{1}{60}$

   G $\frac{1}{120}$ J $\frac{1}{6}$

7. Six different prizes are being awarded to the winners of a contest. In how many different ways can the prizes be awarded?

   A 4,320 ways   C 120 ways

   B 720 ways   D 30 ways

8. Jonathan will have math, English, history, social studies, and science each day next year. What is the probability that his classes will be in alphabetical order?

   F $\frac{1}{5}$ H $\frac{1}{120}$

   G $\frac{1}{24}$ J $\frac{1}{720}$

          Holt McDougal Mathematics

LESSON 12-1

Problem Solving

Solving Two-Step Equations

Write the correct answer.

1. Last week, Carlie had several rice cakes and 3 granola bars as snacks. The snacks contained a total of 800 calories. If each granola bar had 120 calories and each rice cake had 40 calories, how many rice cakes did she have?

2. Jo eats 2,200 calories per day. She eats 450 calories at breakfast and twice as many at lunch. If she eats three meals with no snacks, which meal will contain the most calories?

3. Erika is following a 2,200 calorie-per-day diet. She eats the recommended 9 servings of breads and cereals, averaging 120 calories per serving. She also eats 5 servings of vegetables. If the rest of her daily intake is 870 calories, what is the average number of calories in each serving of vegetables?

4. Brandon follows a 2,800 calorie-per-day diet. He has 11 servings of breads and cereals, which average 140 calories each. Yesterday, he had a combined 9 servings of fruits and vegetables, averaging 60 calories each. How many 180-calorie servings of meat and milk did he have to complete his diet?

Choose the letter for the best answer.

The table shows calories burned by a person performing different activities.

5. Kamisha swims for 0.25 hour. How many calories does she burn?

   A 30 calories   C 1.95 calories

   B 195 calories   D 117 calories

6. Stu jogs at a rate of 5 mi/h. How far must he jog to burn 418.5 calories?

   F 9 mi   H 3.75 mi

   G 4.65 mi   J 45 mi

7. Terry rides her bike for 40 minutes and plays basketball for an hour. How many calories does she burn?

   A 67 calories   C 670 calories

   B 560 calories   D 1,300 calories

Calories Used in Activities

Activity	Calories (per min)
Basketball	7.5
Cycling (10 mi/h)	5.5
Jogging	9.3
Swimming	7.8

8. How many hours would you have to ride your bike at 10 mi/h to burn 550 calories?

   F 1.67 hr   H 1.0 hr

   G 1.5 hr   J 0.75 hr

Holt McDougal Mathematics

Problem Solving
Solving Multi-Step Equations

Write the correct answer.

To convert a temperature from degrees Fahrenheit to degrees
Celsius, you can use the formula $(°F - 32)0.56 = °C$.

1. The record high temperature in North Carolina is 110 °F. What is the record high in degrees Celsius?

2. The record low temperature in Florida is –2 °F. What is the record low in degrees Celsius?

3. The record high temperature in the United States is 134 °F. This was recorded in Greenland Ranch, California, on July 10, 1913. What is that temperature in degrees Celsius?

4. The record high in Texas is 120 °F. The record low in Texas is –23 °F. In degrees Celsius, what is the range between the record high and low temperatures in Texas?

5. When the temperature is 4 °C, you need to wear a heavy coat. Write 4 °C in degrees Fahrenheit.

6. When the temperature is 28 °C, you might want to go to the beach. Write 28 °C in degrees Fahrenheit.

Choose the letter for the best answer.

7. Faith spent $78 at Fashion Warehouse. She bought 2 shirts that each cost $17.50 and a pair of shoes. How much did she spend for the shoes?

   A $34.00   C $60.50

   B $43.00   D $113.00

8. Three friends each pay $4.15 to buy a pizza. A basic pizza costs $9.45. Additional toppings cost $1 each. How many toppings were on the pizza?

   F 2 toppings   H 4 toppings

   G 3 toppings   J 5 toppings

9. Todd buys 3 CDs at $16.99 each and a DVD that costs $24.99. He pays with a $100 bill. How much change does he receive?

   A $24.04   C $49.03

   B $8.04   D $67.96

10. Marina bought 4 books. José bought half as many books as Ben bought. Together, the 3 friends bought 13 books. How many books did Ben buy?

   F 9 books   H 3 books

   G 6 books   J 2 books

LESSON
12-3

Problem Solving

Solving Equations with Variables on Both Sides

Write the correct answer.

1. Five added to twice Erik's age is the same as 3 times his age minus 2. How old is Erik?

2. Three times the perimeter of a triangle is the same as 75 decreased by twice the perimeter. What is the perimeter of the triangle?

3. The area of a pentagon increased by 27 is the same as four times the area of the pentagon, minus 15. What is the area of the pentagon?

4. To repair body damage on a car, AutoBody charges $125, plus $18 per hour. CarCare charges $200, plus $12 per hour. Determine the number of hours for which the two body shops will cost the same.

Choose the letter for the best answer.

5. Sandy and Suzanne are planting flower pots around the school building. Sandy has planted 33 pots and is planting at the rate of 10 pots per hour. Suzanne has planted 25 pots and is planting at the rate of 14 pots per hour. In how many hours will they have planted the same number of flower pots?

   A 3 hr   C 2 hr

   B 2.5 hr   D 1 hr

6. The length of the sides of a square measure $2x - 5$. The length of a rectangle measures $2x$, and the width measures $x + 2$. For what value of x is the perimeter of the square the same as the perimeter of the rectangle?

   F $x = 2$ H $x = 10$

   G $x = 7$ J $x = 12$

7. Louisa used Downtown Taxi, which charges $2 for the first mile and $1.10 for each additional mile. Pietro used Uptown Cab, which charges $5 for the first mile and $0.95 for each additional mile. They paid the same amount and traveled the same distance. How far did they travel?

   A 25 mi   C 20 mi

   B 21 mi   D 15 mi

8. Toni bought some beach towels on sale for $8 each. Theo bought the same number of beach towels at the full price of $12. Toni's total was $24 less than Theo's total. How many beach towels did they each buy?

   F 6 towels   H 9 towels

   G 8 towels   J 12 towels

LESSON 12-4	**Problem Solving**
	Inequalities

Write the correct answer.

The American College of Sports Medicine recommends exercising at an intensity of 60% to 90% of your maximum heart rate.

Heart Rates by Age

Age	Maximum Heart Rate	Target Range
20–24	200	120–180
25–29	195	117–176
30–34	190	114–171
35–39	185	111–167
40–44	180	108–162

1. Mara is 25 years old. Write a compound inequality to represent her target heart rate range while bike riding.

_____

2. Leia is 38 years old. Write a compound inequality to represent the zone between her maximum heart rate and the upper end of her target range.

_____

3. Rudy is 42 years old. Write an inequality to represent at least 70% of his maximum heart rate.

_____

4. Write a compound inequality to represent 60% to 90% of your maximum heart rate in ten years.

_____

Choose the letter for the graph that represents each statement.

5. Alena decided to pay not more than $25 to get her old bike repaired.

  A I   C III

  B II   D IV

6. It was so cold last week that the temperature never reached 25 °F.

  F I   H III

  G II   J IV

I. ←|——|——|——|——|——⊕——|——|——|——|——|→
   0 5 10 15 20 25 30 35 40 45 50

II. ←|——|——|——|——|——⊕——|——|——|——|——|→
   0 5 10 15 20 25 30 35 40 45 50

III. ←|——|——|——|——|——●——|——|——|——|——|→
   0 5 10 15 20 25 30 35 40 45 50

IV. ←|——|——|——|——|——●——|——|——|——|——|→
   0 5 10 15 20 25 30 35 40 45 50

7. There were at least 25 people ahead of Ivan in the cafeteria line.

  A I   C III

  B II   D IV

8. The garden yielded more than 25 pounds of potatoes.

  F I   H III

  G II   J IV

           Holt McDougal Mathematics

LESSON
12-5

Problem Solving

Solving Inequalities by Adding or Subtracting

Write the correct answer.

1. A small car averages up to 29 more miles per gallon of gas than an SUV. If a small car averages 44 miles per gallon, what is the average miles per gallon for an SUV?

_____

2. Carlos is taking a car trip that is more than 240 miles, depending on the route he chooses. He has already driven 135 miles. How much farther does he have to go?

_____

3. Driving into the city usually takes 25 minutes. If there is a lot of traffic, the trip can take up to 45 minutes. How much additional time should you allow during a heavy traffic period?

_____

4. To qualify for the heavyweight wrestling division, Kobe must weigh at least 180 pounds. If Kobe weighs 168 pounds now, how much weight should he gain?

_____

Choose the letter for the best answer.

5. On one day, the range of temperatures in one state was at most 27°. If the lowest temperature in the state was 59°, what was the highest temperature?

   A $t > 86°$ C $t = 86°$

   B $t \leq 86°$ D $t \geq 86°$

6. The highest possible score on the Scholastic Aptitude Test is 2,400. Rebecca scored 1,780. She needs a score of at least 1,950 to qualify for a scholarship. How much higher must her score be?

   F $s \leq 170$ H $s \geq 170$

   G $s \leq 450$ J $s \geq 450$

7. Romero is saving to buy an Apex Model 12 Computer. The lowest price that Romero can find for the computer is $1,250. Romero now has $825. His grandmother is going to give him another $200. How much more money does Romero need?

   A $x < \$225$ C $x \geq \$225$

   B $x < \$425$ D $x \geq \$425$

8. The seating capacity of the school gym is 550. So far, there are 210 fans at a basketball game. How many more fans could attend the game?

   F $f \geq 340$

   G $f > 210$

   H $f \leq 340$

   J $f < 340$

LESSON
12-6

Problem Solving

Solving Inequalities by Multiplying or Dividing

Write the correct answer.

1. U.S. Postal Service regulations state that a package can be mailed using Parcel Post rates if it weighs no more than 70 pounds. What is the maximum number of books weighing 12 pounds each that can be mailed in one box using Parcel Post rates?

2. Marc wants to buy a set of at least 6 antique chairs for his dining room. He has decided to spend no more than $390. What is the most he can spend per chair?

3. Alfonso earns $9.00 per hour working part-time as a lab technician. He wants to earn more than $144 this week. At least how many hours does Alfonso have to work?

4. Mrs. Menendez invited 8 children to her son's birthday party. She wants to make sure that each child gets at least 4 small prizes. At least how many prizes should she buy?

Choose the letter for the best answer.

5. The Computer Club spent $2,565 on mouse pads. The members plan to sell the mouse pads during the book fair. If they charge $9.50 for each mouse pad, how many must they sell in order to make a profit?

   A $n \leq 271$ C $n \geq 271$

   B $n \leq 270$ D $n \geq 270$

6. The Parents Organization bought 1,000 bumper stickers at $1.25 each to sell at football games. They want to make at least $750 profit. What should be the selling price of the bumper stickers?

   F $p \geq \$1.25$ H $p \geq \$1.75$

   G $p \geq \$1.50$ J $p \geq \$2.00$

7. In 2000, the national ratio of students to computers with Internet access in public schools was 7:1. Winston School had 623 students. If the school had a lower ratio, how many computers with Internet access did Winston School have?

   A $c \geq 90$ C $c \geq 91$

   B $c \leq 90$ D $c \leq 91$

8. A new theme park averaged fewer than 2,000 visitors per week during the winter months. What was the average daily attendance?

   F $a \geq 290$ H $a > 385$

   G $a \leq 186$ J $a < 286$

Holt McDougal Mathematics

LESSON	**Problem Solving**
12-7	*Solving Multi-Step Inequalities*

Write the correct answer.

1. Grace earns $7 for each car she washes. She always saves $25 of her weekly earnings. This week, she wants to have at least $65 in spending money. At least how many cars must she wash?

_____

2. Monty has saved $400 to spend on a video game player and games. The player he wants costs $275. The games each cost $39. At most, how many games can he buy along with the player?

_____

3. A video game club charges $8 per month as a membership fee, plus $2.75 for each game rental. Eugenie plans to join and rent no more than 5 games a month. What amount should she budget each month for video games?

_____

4. Cooper Middle School has a goal of collecting more than 1,000 cans of food in a food drive. So far, 375 cans have been collected. During the last 13 days of the drive, at least how many cans must be collected each day in order to meet the goal?

_____

Choose the letter for the best answer.

5. In January 2005, it cost $0.37 to mail a letter weighing up to 1 ounce. Each additional ounce or part of an ounce cost $0.23. At most, what is the weight of a letter with $1.06 in postage?

   A $w < 4$ oz   C $w \leq 4$ oz

   B $w < 3$ oz   D $w \leq 3$ oz

6. Martin is planning a hedge along the back of his yard. The total length can be no more than 23 feet, and he will put a 4-foot-wide gate in the hedge. Each plant needs 2.5 feet of space to grow properly. How many plants should he buy?

   F $n \leq 7$ H $n \leq 9$

   G $n < 7$ J $n < 9$

7. The 12 members of the Middle School filmmaking club need to raise at least $1,400 to make a short film. They already have raised $650. How much more should each member raise on average?

   A $x \geq \$62.50$ C $x < \$62.50$

   B $x \leq \$62.50$ D $x > \$62.50$

8. The rule of thumb in filmmaking is that you must shoot at least 3 minutes of film for every minute in a movie's "final cut." A 30-minute roll of film costs $250. How much will film cost to make a 90-minute movie?

   F $c \geq \$22,500$ H $c \leq \$67,500$

   G $c \leq \$7,500$ J $c \geq \$2,250$

    Holt McDougal Mathematics